pot it **grow it** eat it

pot it **grow it** eat it

home-grown produce | from pot to pan

kathryn hawkins

NEW
HOLLAND

Published in 2010 by New Holland Publishers (UK) Ltd
London · Cape Town · Sydney · Auckland
www.newhollandpublishers.com

Garfield House, 86–88 Edgware Road,
London W2 2EA, United Kingdom

80 McKenzie Street, Cape Town 8001, South Africa
Unit 1, 66 Gibbes Street, Chatswood, NSW 2067, Australia
218 Lake Road, Northcote, Auckland, New Zealand

10 9 8 7 6 5 4 3 2 1

A catalogue record for this book is available from
the British Library

ISBN 978 1 84773 665 9

Senior Editor: Corinne Masciocchi
Design: Simon Daley
Photography: Stuart MacGregor and Ian Garlick
Production: Laurence Poos
Editorial Direction: Rosemary Wilkinson

Reproduction by Modern Age Repro House Ltd, Hong Kong
Printed and bound by Times Offset (M) Sdn Bhd, Malaysia

Contents

Introduction

I first started growing plants in containers when I lived in a flat in London. We had a communal garden, and being on the ground floor I had easy access to the outside space. I was fortunate to have a south-facing wall adjoined to my flat which was marvellous for growing tender crops, and they never once got caught in a frost in the 12 years I lived there. I used to grow mostly salads, tomatoes, herbs and fruit, as well as Mediterranean shrubs like mimosa and oleander; I was also able to put my lemon tree outside all summer long without fear of harm from adverse weather conditions. In fact, coming to think about it, I was very spoilt indeed; I didn't even have to remember to water my plants regularly, because my two garden-loving neighbours were much more diligent with the watering can than I was! A few years on, I have my own garden and live in mid Scotland. I still grow quite a few crops in containers, mostly for convenience, as containers enable me to grow crops that wouldn't suit my soil conditions or which spread like wild fire if not contained; it also means I can quickly move things if adverse weather conditions prevail. I especially like grow bags: they suit my practical (and slightly impatient) nature because you can just open them up and start planting straight away. I enjoy being outside and tinkering around, looking after my plants; I find it therapeutic and relaxing, and it's so easy to keep container plants neat and tidy with just a few simple tweaks here and there.

Our interest in gardening has been on the increase over the past few years, and most recently we've been reminded of the health and planet-saving benefits of growing our own fruit and vegetables. Most people think they have to have their own garden or outside space to raise crops successfully, but it's really not the case. It may be surprising to discover that just about anyone with as little space as a narrow window ledge can raise their own produce. This is the book that will help you find something to plant, grow, and then eat and enjoy, no matter how much space you have.

A wide selection of fruit, herbs and vegetables can be grown indoors and outside; from herbs, chilli peppers, cherry tomatoes and strawberries on the windowsill, to small trees and root vegetables in a patio or balcony trough. Apart from customizing your own planters, tubs and pots, garden centres sell plenty of specialized containers for growing your crops, in every conceivable shape, colour, size and material, and to suit all budgets. You'll also find grow-your-own kits for raising produce like potatoes in a sack, salad in a bag, or mushrooms in a box. You will need to do a bit of careful planning before you get started and I've set out all the things you should take into account before you begin, but once you've got past the first few pages of this book, you'll be itching to get going! Then, almost as if by magic, within a few weeks you'll quite literally be able to enjoy the fruits of your labour, and will no doubt be feeling very pleased with yourself as you tuck into your first plate of home-grown produce. In case you need a bit of inspiration, I've included a few recipe ideas at the back of the book to give you some suggestions on how to make the most of your produce.

Container gardening is great fun and can really capture your imagination and help liven up the smallest of spaces with a splash of colour from a jazzy pot, fresh foliage and, not forgetting, of course, an abundance of healthy-looking, great-tasting, home-grown, quality produce. So get your potting gloves on and get planting!

Bon appétit!

Kathryn Hawkins

Practicalities of container gardening

The advantages of container growing are manifold, but you do need to stretch your imagination and be a bit creative if you think you haven't got enough of the right kind of space. If you haven't got much ground space, think about vertical growing: how about containers on steps or stacked on different levels of bricks or stone? And don't forget hanging baskets, windowsills and ledges. If you have no outside space at all, have a look around your living space and see what sills and ledges could be used indoors, and whether you could position tables or other units nearer to the window to enable you to grow more. Containers offer easy and instant access to your crops, and help bring the outside indoors. You can move plants around easily to get as much sun as possible or into the shade and shelter when necessary, and once they're up and running most plants require only simple routine maintenance.

Containers can brighten up any 'dead space' and are ideal for hiding anything unsightly; in fact they can add a feature to the dullest-looking wall or fence. You can change things around as often as you like to make up endless pot-scapes. Above all else, I think container growing can offer anyone the chance to raise their own produce and give real satisfaction in the process.

Before you go out and buy containers have a careful think about the space you've got and what you might want to grow. Most crops need some sunshine, but not all like full sun, and some need protection from strong heat, wind and frosts. You'll also need to be able to water them regularly so think about the practicalities of this – some plants need more water than others. At the same time, think about what you like eating and how much produce you could actually get through – it's pointless trying to grow too much and then have produce wasted. When you've drawn up a list, read through the vegetable, herb and fruit directory on pages 20–103 and check the suitability of your site against your chosen plants (there's a short potted guide on each entry for quick reference).

Take some measurements of the space you have and work out how many pots you might need, then make a rough plan of where they might go. There will be plenty of choice of pots in all shapes and sizes, so you should be able to fill even the most abstract of spaces with something. At any largish garden centre you'll find pots and containers available to suit all

◀ Gardener's favourite: traditional terracotta pots.

pockets and tastes, from the practical and cheap plastics and fibreglass, to the more traditional wood and terracotta. Then there are colourful glazed and patterned earthenware pots, stone and concrete ware, and finally, trendy metal and slate, plus plenty of combinations in between. For a really cheap and practical solution, choose grow bags or simply roll down the top of a bag of compost and use that as a planter. And if you want to improvise and recycle, then the world's your oyster providing you can make draining holes in it, and don't forget second-hand pots and planters can always be given a new lease of life by varnishing, painting, stencilling or sticking on mosaics to pretty them up.

Here are a few other things to consider apart from cost when shopping for containers:

- **Size-v-space** Always choose the biggest container you can afford for the money and the space you have. Depth and width are more important for certain plants, but as a general rule, the bigger the better. Remember the weight of the container when it is planted – this may be a factor especially if you have a balcony, or you want to be able to move things around.
- **Drainage** Make sure whatever you choose has ready-made holes in the bottom or can be drilled easily to make your own.
- **Porosity** Terracotta and wood are more porous than plastics or glazed pots, and have a tendency to dry out quickly; they may not be the best choice if you are not on hand to water regularly. However, this can be minimized by lining the pots with plastic, or wood can be sealed with varnish.
- **Self-watering** If watering is going to be difficult to maintain, it is worth investigating self-watering containers. These are usually made of plastic, can be quite costly and don't always look good, but they are certainly a practical solution. You can also find kits to help transform other types of container into self-watering ones.
- **Heat retention** Some materials like metal will subject plant roots to extremes of temperature in the heat and cold, so look at lining them to help make them more plant friendly – bubble wrap is a good liner in this instance. You can also use thick

plastic sheeting like pond liner, or remnants of a compost bag, or wads of garden fleece.

- **Length of life** If something's cheap it's probably not going to last that long. This is fine for produce that has only a short life, but long-living trees and bushes should be put in containers that are sturdy and frost proof and will last the lifetime of the plant. One last point: remember, if you choose an expensive container because it's fashionable, first weigh up its practicality for your requirements and then think about whether you'll get fed up with looking at it after a few months.

More ideas…

With so many things to think about already, your brain is probably fit to burst! Or you might be feeling a bit fed up because you think you can't grow as much as you thought. In such situations, I usually find a simple brainstorming session gets me back on track. Think about combination planting (where you can put together several plants in one area that all complement each other in some way). A small but sunny situation could lend itself perfectly to an Oriental 'pot garden' of garlic, coriander, spring onions, chillies and pak choi – all the ingredients for one sensational flavoursome meal. If you like Italian, combine pepper and tomato plants with basil and rocket. Try mixing the seeds of different salad leaves with edible flowers and soft-leaved herbs in a large container for a pick-and-come-again salad bowl idea. If you haven't got any shade, you could think about planting a small fruit tree or bush in a container with a wide circumference, then underneath in the shade of the foliage you can plant more shallow-rooted crops that are quicker to mature and don't like too much direct sunlight. Strong-stemmed, more mature trees and bushes can also be used as natural support systems for climbing plants like runner beans, and tall varieties of sweetcorn can be used as natural support structures for peas, broad beans and French beans as their root system is shallow enough not to disturb the growing corn. For the fruit lover, a hanging basket of strawberries or a window-ledge container of the alpine varieties makes an easy and satisfying choice.

Getting started

This is an important section to read before buying your seeds and seedlings. Reading these points will help save you money and avoid wasted purchases, and above all, will help you get the best results possible.

Selecting seeds, seedlings and specimen plants

Once you've got an idea of what you want to grow, you'll be looking around for seeds and seedlings. Like food products, seeds have a sell-by date, so always check they are in date before purchase. Go to a reputable garden centre or seed merchant that has a quick turnover of products, and make sure the packets are completely intact and undamaged. Pre-packaged seeds are treated so that you don't introduce anything other than the seed at the time of planting – seeds from friends or unknown sources will not have this guarantee so you never quite know what else you might have to deal with. Many seed merchants have a money-back guarantee, so if their seeds don't germinate, you won't be completely out of pocket. Think about a space you can use for sowing seeds as you'll need it to fill and store seed trays until seedlings are big enough to 'pot up' into bigger containers.

When it comes to seedlings and specimen plants, it's really down to common sense. A garden centre or nursery with a good reputation will make sure their plants are well watered and look healthy, and some offer guarantees against failure. Don't buy anything that's withered or damaged, or excessively dry, or that looks like it's out-grown its pot.

Choosing the correct growing medium

You've got your pot at the ready, now what do you fill it with? There are certainly plenty of substances available to choose from, but for the container gardener you can get away with between one and five types, depending on what you are planning to grow:

- **Seed compost** Necessary if you're planning on germinating plants from seed. It is fine textured and contains the right balance of nutrients necessary to get seeds germinated and keep them in good condition for about six weeks.
- **Soil-based compost** Best suited to plants that will be in a container for a long time, such as fruit trees. It is a heavy-textured mixture which is able to retain water and nutrients for a longer period of time than other composts. If you fill a container with only soil-based compost, it will be heavy and dense, therefore it is usually lightened by adding a quantity of soil-less compost or other material to improve drainage and texture.
- **Soil-less or general- (multi-) purpose compost** Most widely used and readily available. Traditionally made from composted peat, but now mostly from peat substitutes. It is not always advisable to buy the cheapest compost, as with most things, you get what you pay for, and quality costs. A good-quality general-purpose compost should contain sufficient nutrients to feed your plants for six weeks. General-purpose compost is much lighter in texture than those containing soil and subsequently it will dry out more quickly; frequent watering is, therefore, essential.
- **Ericaceous compost** Necessary for growing acid-loving plants like blueberries and cranberries. It is a lime-free mixture that will help prevent acid-loving plants developing chlorosis (see page 18). To retain acid levels, water only with rainwater, and choose lime-free plant food when feeding.
- **Citrus compost** A special blend of nutrients in a compost mix that's ideally suited to all members of the citrus family and their close relatives.

All composts lose their potency once exposed to the air, so keep opened bags well sealed, and only buy in quantities that can be used up quickly.

Container drainage

To ensure nutrients are retained in the compost for your growing plants and that they can take up water without drowning, it is important to make sure your container is prepared properly with drainage material. Adding horticultural grit to a compost can improve drainage if it seems a bit wet and sticky and holds together in clumps. You'll see a substance called 'vermiculite' on sale in the garden centre which can be mixed into compost to make it lighter and improve aeration – this is a good substance to use if you're trying to reduce the weight of a pot on a balcony.

Before you fill your container with compost, make sure there are sufficient drainage holes. Cover the bottom entirely with drainage material. Things to use could be pieces of old, broken terracotta pot, gravel or small stones. If you want to keep the weight down, you can use polystyrene chips or small upturned plastic flowerpots over large holes. All these substances will help create a good drainage layer and help prevent waterlogging and do not decompose in water or soil.

Once filled and in position, keep containers slightly off the ground so that excess water can drain away and the pot is unable to 'sit' in a puddle of water. Either use bricks or special pot feet which sit neatly under the edge of the bottom of pots to keep the air circulating underneath.

Feeding your plants

In a garden bed or border, plants can send their roots down deep into the soil for extra nutrition, but container-grown specimens are completely reliant on what you feed them. Compost provides food for six weeks, then after this it's up to you to carry on providing your plants with food and nutrition so that they can develop properly and provide you with a good crop. Not all crops require additional feeding; salad leaves, which are quick to mature, don't need additional feeding, but plants which have a long, steady growing season, like tomatoes, require lots of food. There are several organic and non-organic ways you can feed your plants, and it's up to personal preference which you choose. Soluble fertilizers are mixed into

▲ **A specialist 'drip feed' for citrus plants.**

water and are fed to plants as you water them. This fertilizer is usually required every 10 to 14 days, and is often applied to fleshy fruits like tomatoes, cucumbers and courgettes. Other types come in the form of granules which are mixed into the compost at the time of planting and slowly release nutrients over a six-week period; you'll also find 'plugs' of these granules which you can push into the compost more easily at a later date when it's time to replenish the food supply.

To increase the yield of flowering and fruiting plants, a fertilizer that's high in potash is required, whilst a nitrogen-rich feed increases the development of foliage so is important for greens. Avoid any fertilizer that contains lime for acid-loving plants as this will act as a neutralizing agent in the compost, and the acidity level will drop. You'll also find plenty of specific compounds for a variety of plants, for example, citrus feeders for pushing into the compost and slowly drip feeding your plant over a period of weeks.

With any plant food you choose, always follow the manufacturer's instructions with regards to dosage and application.

Tools of the trade

The good news for container gardeners is that you don't need much to get going. Take a trip to any garden centre and you'll see an array of gardening tools, whilst some may be useful, you can really make do with just a few basics.

- **Dibber** An inexpensive piece of kit that enables you to make a perfect hole in a pot of compost into which you put a seed or seedling. You can make various depths depending on how far you push the dibber into the compost. Available in different circumferences, ideally buy a slim dibber for seeds and tiny seedlings, and a wider one for bigger specimens. An old pencil or piece of dowling will also do the trick.
- **Trowel and hand fork** Good for getting into small areas and in between plants to weed and turn the compost over. Trowels enable you to make larger holes than a dibber, necessary for planting larger seedlings and specimens, and you don't have to disturb the compost as you would with a spade or large fork. Additionally, I find an old kitchen spoon and fork handy for getting into very small areas without disturbing delicate roots.
- **Labels** Seedlings often look very similar when they first appear so label everything as it is sown so you don't make any mistakes. Make sure you use an indelible pen that won't wash off when you water. Save wooden ice lolly sticks to make your own.
- **Watering can and mister** With a small nozzle or 'rose' for getting right to the base of your potted plants. I prefer to use different-size cans for different tasks, but it depends on storage space. For instance, I have a can for rainwater and one for tap water, and another can for applying liquid fertilizer. A plastic water spray with a fine nozzle is perfect for applying a fine mist of tepid water to cool or cleanse your plants, and to help fruit set and encourage a good crop.

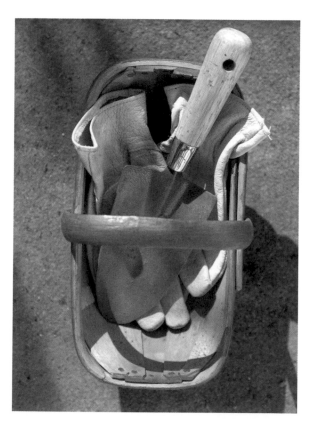

■ **Canes, support systems, string and ties** Bamboo canes are inexpensive and very useful for cutting down to different lengths, depending on what needs supporting. Pop a stopper on the top (or a plastic cup) to prevent any accidents. They can also be tied together with garden string to make more detailed frames, such as a wigwam for runner beans or a trellis system for blackberries – much cheaper than elaborate ready-made structures (although the latter can add an artistic and stylish feature to a small space). Lengths of string can also be tied to canes for adding extra supports to allow peas to entwine themselves on. Collect fine twigs and sticks from hedgerows for adding to pots of peas to give them support. Whilst garden string can be used for securing most plants, you may prefer to use plastic ties or clips for smaller or more fragile plants (you'll find quite a selection at your garden centre).

■ **Secateurs and scissors** Probably one of the biggest gardening tool expenses, but worth it. A decent pair

of secateurs for cutting back and pruning will last you many years if you look after them properly. It's also worth putting aside a pair of kitchen scissors for gardening use as well – useful for 'snipping' away in smaller areas, and for harvesting salad leaves, herbs and soft fruit. Floristry scissors are useful as well.

■ **Fleece and netting** Depending on where you live and what you're planting, you may need to buy some of each. Both are inexpensive and readily available from garden centres, cut to measure from the roll. Easy to store and use, you'll be able to cover your pots and containers quickly in order to protect them from adverse weather conditions, strong sunlight and pests.

■ **Gloves** Gardeners seem to be split 50/50 over whether they wear gloves or not. I can see the attraction of not wearing gloves – you certainly get more of a feel for what you're doing – and for finer tasks I don't wear them. On the whole, I'm a glove wearer (thin latex gloves are useful for most gardening jobs), mainly because I'm in and out of the kitchen cooking as well!

■ **Tamper and riddle** Optional extras, but very useful if you get the gardening bug. A tamper is a block of wood (various sizes and shapes are available) on a handle which is used for firming and levelling compost in seed trays and containers. It is also useful for firming in seedlings and plants. A riddle is really a garden sieve. It comes in different sizes; a small one is used for sieving compost finely over seeds, or for getting any lumps or stones out of compost.

■ **Pot decorations** I'm including these because I'm amazed at just how many bits and pieces you can buy to jazz up your pots. From simple windmills that turn in the wind (they make good bird scarers), to pebbles and glass chippings to sprinkle over the compost (also acting as a mulch), to highly decorative statues and structures for pushing in and around your pots, just to add a bit of fun or a splash of colour to an ordinary-looking container.

◀ **Some of my gardening essentials: bamboo canes, gloves, trug and trowel, string and secateurs.**

Tips and techniques when planting from seed

Many seeds need to be germinated before they can be planted in a container, and some need the extra warmth of the indoors to get started. You'll find all sorts of plastic seed trays, single pots and modules for raising seedlings. Biodegradable or 'peat' pots are the most convenient because once the seedling has developed the whole pot is planted – ideal for crops like sweetcorn which don't like their roots disturbed. You'll find plenty of ready-made biodegradable pots on offer in an assortment of sizes, but look out for 'peat pellets' which expand to form self-contained modules once water is applied – perfect if you don't have much storage space. For tender crops like peppers and chillies, you should use pots or trays with a propagator lid or clear plastic covering to retain as much warmth as possible in order to assist germination. I use a sheet of clingfilm over the top of trays to get seeds established, and then change to a domed lid as the seedlings grow. If finding a warm spot is a problem, you may need to invest in a heated propagator to help speed things along but these can be costly so investigate first (I've managed to raise all my seedlings for this book without an electric propagator and I live in a chilly Victorian stone villa!).

More specific growing instructions are given under the entries in the vegetable, herb and fruit directory for each plant (see pages 20–103), but the basic principles are the same. You should fill the seed modules to the top with seed compost, level off the surface by pulling a piece of flat wood over the top and then tap the trays on the work surface to compact the compost. You can then make a hole in the centre of each module using a fine dibber, and drop a few seeds in each (larger seeds can be planted individually). I often use a wetted cocktail stick to transfer individual seeds. Alternatively, if appropriate, lightly scatter seeds across the surface of the tray or pot. Sprinkle the top lightly with a little more fine compost and water with a fine droplet nozzle; this will naturally level off the surface. Label the seed trays and keep in a warm, light position until they germinate, watering to prevent them drying out, and covering with a propagation lid if necessary. As your seedlings grow,

you will probably need to protect them from bright sunlight. You will also need to pot them into bigger, deeper pots so they can establish a better root system before they go outside; this is called 'potting on'. Choose the strongest specimens each time and follow the instructions under Transplanting seedlings and use a general-purpose compost.

Once your seedlings have reached the desired size, it will be a bit of a shock for them when they first get put outside; this must be done gradually so that they get used to the temperature change: this is called 'acclimatizing' or 'hardening off'. Once seedlings reach the desired size and the temperature outside is favourable, put them in a sheltered place, avoiding wind, strong sunlight and the risk of frost. Keep them warm and watered, and within a few days they will be ready for planting in your chosen containers.

For outdoor seed raising, choose a small area that is warm and sheltered. You can either raise seedlings

▼ A basic propagation tray with lid.

in trays or modules as previously stated, or if you have space, use larger containers and raise seedlings in short rows until large enough to transplant; alternatively, they can be sown directly into the container you wish to keep them in. Remember that outside seedlings will encounter pests as well as adverse weather conditions, so careful monitoring is essential. Once the seedlings have reached the desired size, they can either be carefully removed and transplanted into another growing container, or maintained in situ.

When seeds are tiny, they are difficult to sow individually. Whilst you should try to sow them thinly, it is inevitable that some will get sown in clumps. When this happens, wait until the seedlings become large enough to handle, then gently pluck out the excess until you have the required density left behind. The 'thinnings', or removed seedlings, are fragile and are best discarded.

Transplanting seedlings

Once you've raised your seedlings to their required size, they're ready for transplanting. Use a small trowel or old kitchen spoon to remove the seedling from the seed tray or module, taking care not to damage the root. If possible, it is better to hold it by the leaves. Make a hole in your chosen container and gently drop the seedling into it. Firm the compost carefully round the seedling and water. This is the same procedure for planting out ready-grown seedlings from the garden centre or nursery. Some plants, like cabbages and rhubarb, need to be supported by the compost after planting. Depending on the size of the plant and the area you have to work in, you can either push the compost down with your foot, hand, a tamper or similar, or the end of a trowel.

Specialist techniques

'Earthing-up' is a technique that helps the underground tubers of root vegetables develop properly, by keeping them out of the light. It also gives stability to top-heavy plants like cabbages and is used to give some plants more support if conditions are windy. First, carefully fork up the compost on top of the container and

remove any weeds. Using a trowel, draw up the compost and pile it against the plant stems to gradually produce a mound with a flattish top, to either cover the shoots or pile up sufficiently to increase support against the stem. You'll probably need to add more compost to the container as well in order to achieve a good result. Repeat this process as the foliage develops until the plant reaches maturity.

Some plants take longer to mature than others. Slow growers include cabbages, garlic and shallots. **Catch cropping** means that you can sow quicker-maturing crops like spinach, chard, baby beetroot, turnips and small carrots around and about the slow growers, and make the most of the container space. **Successive planting** is another useful practice for quick-growing produce that matures at the same time and doesn't keep long, for example lettuces, spring onions, radishes and small carrots. In a container, sow a few seeds in two-weekly stages, and that way you can stagger your harvests throughout the summer.

Taller-growing fruit and vegetable plants often don't have strong stems to support themselves and their produce, so they need another type of **support system**. Depending on what you're growing, you can use simple bamboo canes or more elaborate purpose-built frames. The plant is secured to the support by garden string, special plant ties or clips. Supports are usually put in before the plants get established so that the root system isn't damaged at a later stage, and to encourage plants to grow up the support as they develop.

Moisture is lost from the compost due to the sun's rays and the wind, and in container gardening evaporation is quicker because the sides of the pot are exposed, giving a greater surface area; roots are also more at risk from the elements in a container. You can help retain moisture and help protect roots by applying a 'mulch' of loose-textured material to the top of your compost. Mulch can also be used as a protection against a light frost, and it can help keep weeds down. There are various substances to choose from, such as loose-textured organic matter like less well-rotted compost or coarse bark chippings, and mulches that won't decompose such as glass or slate chippings, gravel or pebbles. The latter type will also make pots look more attractive, and spiky gravel is less appealing to slithering slugs and snails. Mulching is a must for slow-growing plants that require containing for long periods of time, like fruit trees, but if you are growing leafy plants, salads and herbs which grow and mature quickly or plants that spread and cover the compost with their foliage, mulching is unnecessary.

Whatever mulch you chose, always water your plant before topping with the mulch. Apply a mulch to a depth of no more than 7 cm (3 in) round the base of the plant.

Watering

All container-grown vegetables and fruit need a good, steady supply of water in order to develop and grow properly. Keeping the supply of water consistent is important – feast or famine where water is concerned will result in irregular growth patterns. Containers dry out far more quickly than a traditional soil plant bed because of the larger surface area. Similarly, if a container has poor drainage, it will retain water and become waterlogged causing leaves to yellow and droop. Checking the compost by rubbing it through your fingers is the best way to determine whether it is dry or wet.

You can't rely on the rain to give your plants enough water – raindrops often bounce off foliage leaving the compost below dry. Whilst you might be able to get away with the occasional missed watering, there will come a point when your plants won't rejuvenate; it is important to get into a proper watering routine. Remember that some plants prefer rainwater, and with water shortages, water meters and 'saving the planet' in mind, where possible try to capture some rainwater for your plants in buckets or by installing a water butt.

Use a watering can to get to the base of the plant where water is most needed, and water slowly and thoroughly. Make sure the compost is soaked but not flooded. A light sprinkling of water will be of little use, and flooding an area causes erosion of the compost and its nutrients when the water runs away. In larger containers, you may find it difficult to get in amongst growing plants once they become established so think

about putting a short length of narrow piping with a hole drilled into it in amongst seedlings (usually towards the centre); this way you'll be able to water directly in the pipe and get to where it is most needed without damaging the plants – a perfect solution for plants that require lots of water, like tomatoes and cucumbers.

During hot, dry conditions, you may have to water your plants two or three times a day, depending on where they are sited and what they are planted in – for instance, terracotta is porous and dries out more quickly than a glazed pot. If this is going to be a problem, try to shield containers from the sun when you are not going to be on hand to water them. Also, choose self-watering containers to help reduce the need to water, and try mixing water-retaining granules into the compost before planting. If the worst happens and a plant dries out completely, you may be able to revive it by soaking it in a bucket of water until the compost is completely sodden. Then let it drain and keep it out of strong sunlight for a day or two until it has recovered.

The best time to water is in the morning so that the water has a chance to soak in before the sun gets too hot and causes evaporation. Avoid watering when the sun is too hot otherwise foliage may scorch. There is more chance of spreading pests around if you water too late in the day as the extra moisture in the atmosphere will attract them.

Protecting your crops

Tender young plants can be susceptible to damage from the elements as well as making tempting treats for the feathered, furry and slimy creatures of the outdoors. There are a number of measures you can take to protect them, and you'll find several solutions at a garden centre or DIY store. A cloche is the most traditional method for covering a pot, you'll find purpose-built glass or plastic domes of various sizes that can be put directly over individual plants or for simple pest protection, you can buy netting or fleece covering to put over your own frame. Garden fleece can be used as a gentle covering to protect newly sown seeds or delicate leaves and flowers; it can also help keep the compost warm for germination, yet allows

▲ **Protecting apple blossom with garden fleece.**

rain and light to penetrate. Thicker layering of fleece can help act as a shade against harsh sunlight and wind, but you may need to use a stronger barrier or screen if these elements are a persistent problem. Garden netting helps keep beaks and claws at bay, either by draping over a plant or when applied to a framework.

For slugs and snails, it's a matter of personal preference – humane traps are available, but most commonly, a handful of slug pellets scattered around seedlings at the time of planting is the cheapest and easiest solution. Copper tape available from garden suppliers can be put round the base of pots as a deterrent, and mulches like spiky grit aren't popular with anything slithery.

Pest control

Indoors and outdoors, your crops may succumb to infestation or disease. Careful routine maintenance is the most important way to keep pests and diseases away; keep a regular check on your plants and always remove weeds from the surface of the container compost. Immediately get rid of anything that has become diseased, along with any debris from infected plants to reduce the risk of re-infestation. If you've had a serious problem, make sure you get rid of all the pot contents including the compost, in order to avoid re-infesting future crops. It is always better to use fresh compost whenever you plant a new crop as this will ensure your plants get the best start in life and don't succumb to anything lurking in the compost from a previous occupant. This might seem wasteful, but certain plants will deplete the compost of specific nutrients, which in turn may cause growing difficulties for the next set of specimens.

However, with the best will in the world, sometimes your plants will come under attack and there are all sorts of chemical treatments available, but also some organic compounds you can try. Derris dust, sulphur dust and soft soap spray can be used organically, but they need to be applied regularly and act only on contact with the actual pest or disease. Another organic method is companion planting, where some plants act as a deterrent or magnet to help other plants they are positioned next to, and either way can keep insects from enjoying your produce before you do. Plant garlic and strong-smelling herbs like mint nearby to keep pests like carrot fly away, and parsley will help deter onion fly. The scent of the herb rosemary is believed to help prevent the female root fly from laying her eggs, so plant some near cabbages, carrots and turnips. Some flowering plants can be used to deflect pests from growing vegetables, for example, nasturtiums (*Tropaeolum*) attract aphids and caterpillars, and by planting calendula (*Calendula officinalis*) and 'poached egg plants' (*Limnanthes douglasii*) nearby, they will attract lacewings, hoverflies and ladybirds, which in turn feed on aphids. Marigolds (*Tagetes*) can also help keep whitefly away from your crops.

Common pests and diseases and how to deal with them

- **Aphids (blackfly and greenfly)** are common spring and summer pests. **Blackfly** stunt growth, eat flowers and distort pods. Pinch out the tops of broad beans once four trusses have formed. Greenfly is worse in a dry spring and hot humid weather as they carry viruses and cover plants in thick, sticky dew. Neither type of aphid can really be prevented, but spraying with a suitable insecticide can help, or try companion planting as a deterrent.
- **Birds, mice and squirrels** are attracted to seedlings and soft leaves when other food sources are scarce. Erect netting and pin down well to ensure there are no points of entry. Try bird scarers pushed in and around your pots.
- **Botrytis** can affect all berries by covering them in a dense, grey mould, causing the fruit to rot in wet conditions. Fungicides are available.
- **Brown rot** is a fungus that affects many tree fruits, forming brown, bruised patches and white fungal rings on fruit. Common in summer and during storage. Discard all damaged fruit and remove dead shoots when pruning.
- **Cabbage root fly** manifests itself in the form of blue-tinged, wilting leaves on newly planted seedlings. Insecticides are available. Special discs can be placed at the base of seedling stems before transplanting. Fine netting can stop the flies laying their eggs.
- **Canker (1)** affects root vegetables, turning them black and causing them to rot. Plants should be pulled up and destroyed. Choose a resistant variety.
- **Canker (2)** affects fruit trees by attacking the trunk and branches of a tree, causing bark to shrink and expose the inner wood. The most serious form is bacterial canker which can affect cherry and plum trees causing wood to ooze a gum-like substance. Chemical treatments are available, but seek expert advice.
- **Carrot flies** lay their eggs on foliage, and the resulting maggots burrow into the flesh, causing the roots to rot. Affected roots should be destroyed. Worse in dry conditions.

- **Caterpillars** eat holes in leaves from April to October in hot weather. Sprays are available. Inspect the top and underside of leaves for eggs, and remove and crush any that are found. Cover crops with fine netting to prevent butterflies laying their eggs.
- **Chlorosis** manifests itself in the form of yellowy leaves on acid-loving plants caused by too high a pH level. Check compost acidity level before planting, and use ericaceous compost to increase acidity. Water with rainwater and avoid using fertilizers that contain lime.
- **Club root** causes the roots of the cabbage family to swell. Destroy all plants affected with club root. Improve the drainage of the compost and lime if necessary to help minimize the risk of encouraging the disease. Opt to grow resistant varieties.
- **Codling moths** are caterpillars that feed on flesh around cores of orchard fruit in midsummer. Traps can be used to catch moths before they lay their eggs. Chemical sprays are available.
- **Flea beetle** is a very common problem showing as holes on the leaves of any green vegetable and leaf top, but doesn't affect eating quality. Insecticides are available if you want to use them.

▼ **Aphids: the green, mean, eating machines.**

- **Mildew** comes in two forms: **Downy:** yellow blotches on leaves with a brownish mould on the underside, in damp, cool weather. Pods appear distorted. **Powdery:** white patches on leaves, pods and fruit of sheltered plants in dry weather. Chemical sprays are available for both. Otherwise, destroy affected plants.
- **(Cucumber) Mosaic virus** is a common, serious disease spread by greenfly. Leaves become puckered and mottled with yellow and dark green patches; affected plants wither and die. Destroy the affected plants, then wash hands and tools to prevent transmission. Take anti-greenfly precautions to prevent an attack.
- **Onion flies** lay their eggs on all alliums. As the maggots hatch, they turn bulbs and stems to mush. Attacks occur between May and August, especially if the leaves get bruised. Avoid thinning where possible and destroy infected plants.
- **Onion white rot** is a fungal disease affecting alliums. A white fungus forms as alliums grow and quickly causes rot. Destroy infected plants.
- **Pea thrips** are tiny black or yellow insects that cause silver patches on leaves and pods. Worse in dry, hot weather. Chemical sprays are available; otherwise destroy affected plants.
- **Potato blight** is when the foliage of related plants turn yellow and brown, and begin to curl, causing potatoes to rot and turn to slime. Look for resistant varieties. Always plant potatoes in fresh compost.
- **Raspberry beetles** are small, pale brown beetles that feed on new leaves and flowers of raspberry and blackberry in late May. Spray with derris or chemical sprays.
- **Red spider mites** affect all fruit, indoors and out. Mites suck the sap from leaves, leaving white spots and turning them brown. They are especially prevalent in hot weather. Natural predators, such as ladybirds for example, usually act as a natural pest control, but chemical sprays are also available.
- **Root aphids** attack the roots of green vegetables and cover them with white, powdery damage, particularly in dry weather. Destroy affected plants. Keep plants watered to reduce the risk of an attack and look out for resistant varieties.

▲ **Calendulas and nasturtiums act as natural pest 'deflectors' and look very pretty too!**

- **Scale insects** are flattish discs on the underside of indoor plant leaves, and leave a sticky dew on leaves and stems. Plants eventually stop growing. Chemical sprays are available, which should be used on neighbouring plants too as a precaution.
- **Silver leaf** is a fungal disease affecting many fruits but especially plums. Leaves turn silvery and the upper surface peels away. Infected branches show a brownish stain. To reduce the risk of silver leaf, never prune during the dormant season.
- **Slugs and snails** attack any fleshy leaf and root in wet, damp weather, usually at night time, leaving a slimy trail. Use pellets or other slug traps.
- **Violet root rot** causes possible yellowing of foliage, but often only the roots are affected and show as a mass of purplish threads when pulled. Destroy affected roots.
- **Wasps** are difficult to keep away, but try to pick fruit before it over-ripens and remove any decaying fruit. Place 'honey traps' in another area to keep wasps away from fruit trees.
- **Whitefly** is fast breeding in hot, dry weather. It can affect any plant but loves brassicas and tomatoes, and feeds on plant sap. Chemical or soap-based sprays are available, or try companion planting.

Vegetable, herb and fruit directory

Over the following pages I've concentrated on the most **popular** and **rewarding** crops to grow in **containers**. I hope you enjoy planning your space.

Garlic

(*Allium sativum*)

Garlic has been used as a unique flavouring for centuries, especially in Mediterranean countries. It makes an ideal crop for container gardening because a little goes a long way. Life in the kitchen without garlic would be very dull; it is the key flavouring to many dishes. There's a great variety to choose from: mild and sweet tasting to strong and powerful, small to gigantic-sized bulbs, and white, pink and purple varieties too. Garlic can be eaten fresh (green) or it can be dried and stored for several weeks. Another reason to grow garlic is that its distinct aroma is said to ward off many pests, so growing it will act as a natural deterrent for other crops. Buy 'seed' garlic from a nursery or garden centre and not the greengrocer's to insure it is disease-free and suited to your growing climate.

Planting and siting

- In early spring, choose bulbs with plump cloves. Strip the papery skin from the bulb and split up into cloves. Discard any small cloves. ◀ 1
- Using a dibber or trowel, make shallow holes about 2.5 cm (1 in) deep and 10 cm (4 in) apart in the container for each clove.
- Plant the cloves, flat base-side down, and just cover with compost to the tip of the clove. ◀ 2
- Place the container in a sunny position.
- As the bulbs develop, tie the leaves together with string if they start to bend and droop untidily.

Maintenance

- Keep the container well weeded.
- Water during dry spells.

Possible problems

Garlic is usually trouble-free, but can attract general fungal or viral diseases of the Allium family (see pages 18–9).

Harvesting, storing and freezing

Lift garlic when the foliage turns yellow and starts to die down in late summer – leaving it too long will result in the bulbs drying out. Ease the bulbs from the container by carefully digging round them with a small garden hand fork to avoid damage. For drying, dry the bulbs thoroughly in the sun, preferably covered with straw or garden fleece – a sunny window ledge is ideal. When dry, remove any compost and long roots. Either plait the dried leaves together in bunches, or if you prefer to remove the leaves, put the bulbs in net bags or in trays and discard the leaves. Store in a cool, dry place (the kitchen will be too warm and damp). Stored correctly, dried garlic will keep for several months. Put aside a few good-quality bulbs for replanting the next year. Otherwise, enjoy a milder garlic taste and use it whilst it's still fresh and green.

The flavour of garlic deteriorates with prolonged freezing, so it is best used fresh. If you do freeze a garlicky dish, make sure it is well-wrapped to avoid flavour transfer between food items.

Quick potted guide

CONTAINER Suitable for large containers with a minimum depth of 20 cm (8 in).

PLANT From specially prepared 'cloves' in late February to early spring.

POSITION Sunny position.

SOIL Light, non-acid compost.

HARVEST Late summer.

▶ PRODUCE USED ON PAGES 106–137

Leek

(Allium porrum)

Quick potted guide

CONTAINER Suitable for all containers with a minimum depth of 18 cm (6 in).

PLANT From seed in early to mid spring. Buy seedlings for planting out in late spring and summer.

POSITION Open position.

SOIL Fertile, non-acid compost; good drainage.

HARVEST Early autumn to winter, depending on variety.

Like other members of the Allium family, leeks have been a popular vegetable for hundreds of years, especially in winter months when other home-grown vegetables are scarce. They are an easy-to-grow, robust crop with hardy varieties for winter and early types for late summer, the latter being tall and slim, whilst hardy leek varieties are usually more stocky in size or have bluer-green foliage; there are also mid-season varieties available. Leeks require a long growing season in order to enable them to mature sufficiently, yet young, pencil-slim leeks can be enjoyed as a delicious late spring vegetable in their own right if space is more restricted. Leeks can be raised from seed or from ready-grown seedlings.

Planting and siting

■ Because leeks need a long growing season, start them as early in the season as possible. You will need two outdoor containers. Make a drill about 1 cm (½ in) deep in any outdoor container in late March, when the compost is workable and warm enough to permit germination, and sow the leek seeds thinly.

- When the seedlings are about 10 cm (4 in) tall, they are ready for transplantation to your chosen container. Carefully remove from the growing container and trim the tops and roots down. ▶ 1
- Using a dibber, make holes 10 cm (4 in) deep and 15 cm (6 in) apart – closer if you want small, thin leeks – in the compost of your final container. Drop the young leeks into the holes. ▶ 2
- Do not replace any compost, simply fill with water, allowing the compost to naturally settle around the roots. Planting holes will fill naturally over time. ▶ 3
- For ready-grown seedlings, follow steps 1 to 3.

Maintenance

- Keep the containers free from weeds.
- Make sure the leeks are kept watered during dry weather.
- As the plants develop, gradually draw compost up the lower stems in order to keep them white.

Possible problems

Generally trouble-free, however, leeks can be susceptible to any of the problems affecting the Allium family (see pages 18–9).

Harvesting, storing and freezing

Leeks are best harvested before they get too large, when they are about 2 cm (³/₄ in) thick is ideal. If you begin picking them when they are still quite small, this will help to extend the season. Using a trowel or small garden hand fork, carefully ease the leeks out of the container by loosening the compost around them to avoid breaking them as you pull them out. Leeks can be stored outside in compost and then lifted throughout winter as they are needed. To do this, half-fill a deep pot with compost, lift the leeks and lay them against one side of the pot. Cover the roots and white stems with more compost and pack down gently. Take out the leeks and use when required.

For freezing, slice off the root, cut off the tops of the leaves and remove any tough or damaged outer leaves. Slice down the stem halfway through and prize open. Rinse under cold running water to flush out any trapped compost. Shake well to remove excess water. Cut into 2.5 cm (1 in) lengths. Blanch for 2 minutes, cool and dry well. Pack into rigid containers or freezer bags. Store for up to 12 months. Leeks are quite soft and watery once they have been frozen, so it is a good idea to use the thawing liquid in your recipe for extra flavour.

▶ PRODUCE USED ON PAGES 108 & 126

Onion

Shallot (*Allium cepa* Aggregatum group)

Spring (Salad) onion (*Allium cepa*)

Onions are probably the most widely used of all vegetables in the kitchen, but some take a while to mature. For a faster turnover of space, try quicker-growing shallots and spring onions, rather than larger onions. Shallots are best grown from 'sets' – immature bulbs grown from the seed of the previous season. Shallots grow in a cluster of about five small bulbs and are planted earlier than other varieties of onion. Spring onions are grown from seed or seedlings and are the most refined and quickest-growing members of the onion family; if planted early, they can be ready for pulling in as little as eight weeks. Shallot sets are widely available from seed merchants and garden centres in late winter.

Planting and siting

- Shallots can be planted outside straight into your chosen container in February or March. Plant sets in light compost. ▶ 1
- Push the bulbs in so that they are three-quarters buried, leaving only the tip of the bulb above compost level. Plant 15 cm (6 in) apart. ▶ 2

Quick potted guide

CONTAINER Suitable for all containers with a minimum depth of 15 cm (6 in) for all varieties.

PLANT Shallots from sets in February and March; spring onions from seed mid spring to July.

POSITION Open site.

SOIL Light, non-acid compost.

HARVEST Midsummer (shallots); end of May onwards (spring onions).

- For spring onions, make a drill about 1 cm (½ in) deep in an outside container and sow the seeds thinly in mid spring, then sow at three- to four-week intervals in order to give a successive crop until July. If you sow them finely, there should be no need to thin them out. ▶ 3

Maintenance

- Replant any bulbs that have become dislodged.
- Keep containers weeded, and water in early summer if necessary. Spring onions are best grown quickly in order to prevent the leaves toughening, so water them frequently to encourage growth.
- As they grow, tie shallot leaves together with string if they start to bend and look untidy.

Possible problems

Relatively trouble-free, but can succumb to specific Allium infections (see pages 18–9).

Harvesting, storing and freezing

Shallots are usually ready to harvest in July and August. When the foliage dies back, lift the bulb clusters and dry for a few days. Spread out side by side in a shallow box or tray lined with newspaper and placed in a dry, warm place to continue ripening. Ripening can take days to weeks, depending on variety and storage conditions; the skins dry out and become papery when they are fully ripe. Take care not to bruise the shallots and keep the withering leaves intact for tying in bunches and hanging.

Spring onions do not keep well and are best used as soon as possible after harvesting. Pull spring onions as required when they reach about 20 cm (8 in) high. To store, rinse well and keep in the fridge for two to three days. Spring onions are not worth freezing as they keep so well on their own but can be frozen as part of a cooked dish.

Shallots are usually used fresh but if you do want to freeze them, peel and chop, then put them in a freezer bag or small container, seal well and wrap the outside of the bag or container in a layer of cling film to prevent transmitting odour. Alternatively, peel and leave whole. Blanch for about 3 minutes, then cool and dry before packing and freezing. Use within six months of freezing. Add to soups and casseroles directly from frozen when ready-prepared (peeled and chopped), whilst whole shallots are best semi-thawed before cooking like fresh. Shallots become quite watery once they have been frozen, so use the thawing liquid in your recipe for extra flavour.

▶ PRODUCE USED ON PAGES 106–137

Carrot

(*Daucus carota*)

Home-grown roots eaten fresh out of the ground taste far superior to anything you can buy. Carrots are quick to grow, and round or short and dumpy varieties are the best choice for window boxes and shallow containers. Check root growth versus container depth before choosing a variety; some varieties are resistant to carrot fly which are worth considering also.

Planting and siting

- Carrots are best grown from seed, straight into the container, and are easy to grow in rows in window boxes or trench-style containers.
- Carrot seeds can be planted in outside containers when the compost is warmed to about 7°C (45°F) and there is no risk of frost. Do not add

Quick potted guide

CONTAINER Dwarf varieties are best suited for growing in window boxes and small pots with a minimum depth of 20 cm (8 in).

PLANT Usually grown from seed in mid spring to early summer. Buy seedlings for planting out in late spring/summer.

POSITION Open position; like warmth but not excessive heat.

SOIL Light compost with no extra fertilizer; good drainage.

HARVEST Early summer onwards.

fertilizer at this stage as this may cause the roots to split. Choose a sunny spot to position your container and make a drill about 1 cm ($\frac{1}{2}$ in) deep and sow carrot seeds as thinly as possible. Sift a very thin covering of compost over the top. In wide containers, leave about 15 cm (6 in) between rows. ▶ 1

- For a successive harvest, sow a few more seeds in another row, once the first lot has started to germinate.
- When the seedlings are large enough to handle, thin them out to about 5 to 8 cm (2 to 3 in) apart. Discard the thinnings. Take care with this process, as you can attract carrot fly with the smell of bruised foliage. ▶ 2

Maintenance

- Keep weed-free, but take care not to damage the foliage as this may attract carrot fly.
- You can protect seedlings with a low barrier of netting if necessary to deter carrot fly, but this is quite difficult to erect. Alternatively, look at companion planting by positioning your pot near growing mint or garlic plants (see page 17). ▶ 3
- Water, with care, if the conditions are dry, but too much water causes the roots to split.

Possible problems

The main pest is carrot fly and also violet root rot (see pages 18–9).

Harvesting, storing and freezing

Early short-rooted carrots will be ready for pulling in June and July. They are best eaten as soon out of the ground as possible as small carrots wither quickly. Larger roots will keep in the bottom of the fridge for three to five days.

Small whole scraped carrots freeze well: simply trim off the carrot leaves and the wispy root end, and scrape under cold running water using a kitchen knife. Peel bigger carrots thinly using a vegetable peeler and cut into the desired shape. Blanch for 2 to 3 minutes, depending on thickness, then drain and cool. Either open-freeze on trays for later packing, or pack straight away into freezer bags or rigid containers. Keep for up to 12 months. Cook from frozen for 5 minutes in boiling water or add directly to soups and stews.

▶ PRODUCE USED ON PAGES 111 & 126

Potato

(*Solanum tuberosum*)

Perfect for container growing, potatoes should be grown from disease-free 'seed' potatoes available from garden centres or seed merchants. Potatoes are divided into two categories, earlies and main crop, depending on when they can be planted and harvested. Earlies are divided further into first and second earlies. Different varieties have different cooking qualities, flavours, textures and colour qualities, so have a think about your own requirements to help you decide which one is right for you. Usually, an early variety is a good choice as they tend to have more flavour and are ready sooner. You'll find specific growing containers available for growing potatoes, but you can use anything as long as it's deep enough and keeps out the light.

Planting and siting

- Seed potatoes need to be 'chitted' before planting. Stand the potatoes in modules (or egg boxes), the most rounded end uppermost, so that any sprouts or 'eyes' can grow upwards. Put in a cool, frost-free place which is light but not directly in the sun. In a few weeks, short shoots appear. When the shoots are 2.5 to 5 cm (1 to 2 in) long, they are ready to plant. First earlies need to be planted in early spring, and because there is still a chance of frost, choose a sheltered, sunny spot. Second earlies are planted two weeks later, and main crop later still. ▶ 1
- Fill your container with about 18 cm (7 in) compost, and carefully push in two or three tubers per large container, spaced about 12 cm (5 in) apart, with shoots pointing upwards. A single potato can be grown in a smaller pot in order to achieve one yield at a time. ▶ 2
- Cover with a layer of compost about 12 cm (5 in) deep.
- As the shoots appear, keep covering them with a little more compost until the container is full.

Quick potted guide

CONTAINER Suitable for 30 cm (12 in) wide containers with a minimum depth of 30 cm (12 in).

PLANT From seed potatoes from early to late spring, depending on variety.

POSITION Open, sunny site, once there is no risk of frost.

SOIL Fertile, compost but not freshly fertilized; good drainage.

HARVEST Early summer onwards, depending on variety.

■ When the shoots have reached the top of your container, you'll need to 'earth up' by drawing the compost up the stems of foliage (see page 15) to prevent the tubers being exposed to light, turning them green and poisonous. Discard any tubers that have turned green. ▶ 3

Maintenance

■ Continue 'earthing up' as the foliage grows and develops fully.
■ Water if the conditions are dry, especially for the earlies. This is important once the tubers develop.

Possible problems

Blight is the biggest problem and slugs may also be a nuisance (see pages 18–9).

Harvesting, storing and freezing

Potatoes are not hardy and should be lifted before the first frosts. Early potatoes are ready for harvesting, about 12 weeks after planting. They don't store well and are best enjoyed fresh. In a large container, use a garden hand fork to carefully dig in well below the tubers and lever them out, pulling on the foliage at the same time. For small containers, put some plastic sheeting down before tipping the pots on their side and prizing out the plant. This way you'll be able to spread out the roots to gather your harvest of potatoes, and then gather up the debris for an easy tidy up.

Main crop potatoes are ready for harvesting in the autumn. Remove the foliage about two weeks before harvesting in order to help the skins firm up. Choose a dry, warmish day for harvesting and leave the potatoes to air dry for a couple of hours. Discard any that are damaged or diseased, then pack in thick brown paper potato sacks or hessian bags; tie the top of the bag and keep in a dry, cool, frost-free, dark place for up to three months. Bags should allow air to circulate and prevent light getting in. Check frequently for rot or mould.

For freezing, potatoes should be cooked in the form of boiled whole new potatoes, mashed, roasted or baked in their jackets. All should be cooled, packed and frozen for up to six months and thawed before reheating. Raw potato can be frozen in the form of chips: blanch uncooked chips in boiling water for 1 minute, drain and cool quickly. Open-freeze until solid and then pack into freezer bags. Seal, label and store for up to six months. To use, defrost and cook in hot oil.

▶ PRODUCE USED ON PAGES 110, 118, 125 & 126

Turnip

Brassica napa Rapifera group

including Beetroot (*Beta vulgaris*)

Early and dwarf varieties of turnip grow quickly and can be picked young so are excellent if space is short. They may be grown between slower to mature roots and will be ready for picking long before others. Their foliage will add some much-wanted colour at a time of year when other plants are still developing, and the young leaves can be picked and cooked like spinach. Choose small, round or 'globe' varieties of beetroot for container growing; these can be used for summer and autumn eating, either grated raw or cooked for salads and as a hot vegetable. Small beetroot leaves can be picked off and eaten raw as a slightly earthy-flavoured salad leaf. Turnips and beetroot are usually grown from seed.

Planting and siting

- Beetroot seed usually comes in clusters of seeds (dried whole beetroot) and resembles small pieces of cork. Alternatively, you may find monogerm or single beetroot seed. Soak beetroot seed for a few hours before sowing to speed up germination. ▶ 1
- Plant beetroot seed outside when there is no risk of frost. Make a drill about 2 cm (³/₄ in) deep and sow the seeds about 5 cm (2 in) apart.

Quick potted guide

CONTAINER Suitable for all containers with a minimum depth of 25 cm (10 in).

PLANT From seed in spring to midsummer.

POSITION Fairly sunny site (turnip and beetroot); avoid excessive heat and strong sunlight; avoid frost (beetroot).

SOIL Fertile and non-acid compost (turnip and beetroot); good drainage (beetroot).

HARVEST Mid to late summer (turnip); midsummer to autumn, before the first frosts (beetroot).

- For early and dwarf turnips, make a drill about 1 cm (½ in) deep in an outdoor container and sow the tiny round seeds as thinly as possible. Sprinkle a very thin covering of compost over the top. Leave about 18 cm (7 in) between rows if your container is large enough. Continue to sow at two-week intervals throughout the summer for a continuous supply of small turnips.
- When both types of seedlings are large enough to handle, thin them out to about 7 cm (3 in) apart. Discard the thinnings.

Maintenance

- Weed carefully to avoid damaging the growing roots.
- Water to encourage quick growth and prevent the roots drying out.
- You may need to protect seedlings from birds by erecting netting or other protection (see pages 16–7). ▶ 2
- Try protecting with fleece to shield from strong sunlight as this causes the leaves to wilt.

Possible problems

Turnips can be prone to diseases of the cabbage family such as flea beetles and club root (see pages 18–9). Beetroot are usually trouble-free.

Harvesting, storing and freezing

Pick both roots sooner rather than letting them get too big; for best flavour and texture, roots should be no smaller than the size of a golf ball and no bigger than a tennis ball. They can simply be pulled from the container when required and used as soon as possible. They will keep for two to three days in the fridge: put the roots in a jug of water and leave the foliage on for best results. Take care not to damage beetroot bulbs as they will 'bleed' and stain. ▶ 3

To freeze turnips, choose small roots, and cut off the leafy top and root end. Wash and blanch for 2 minutes, drain, cool and pack into rigid containers or freezer bags. Store for up to 12 months and cook from frozen for 8 to 10 minutes.

To freeze beetroot, choose small roots. Wash well, taking care not to cut into the skin. Place in a saucepan, unpeeled, cover with water, bring to the boil and cook for 1 to 2 hours, depending on size. Rinse in cold water, carefully rub off the skin and pack into freezer bags. Larger roots are better sliced before freezing. Keep in the freezer for up to six months. Defrost for 4 to 6 hours in the fridge before using.

▶ PRODUCE USED ON PAGES 118, 126 & 137

Broccoli and Calabrese

Brassica oleracea Cymosa group and *B. oleracea* Italica group

These familiar mild-tasting green vegetables are now a mainstay of our diet, and are highly regarded nutritionally. Look out for early maturing varieties as traditional types take a long time to grow and would not be the best choice in a limited space. Broccoli and calabrese like a fertile compost to start life (compost enriched with 'green manure' is ideal). They require frequent watering in order to mature and are raised from seed or seedlings.

Planting and siting

- Sow broccoli and calabrese seed directly into outside containers. You will need two separate containers. If you have indoor space, seeds can be raised in modules until big enough to plant out.
- Make sure the compost is rich and fertile, and warmth will help the seeds germinate. Firm gently and make a drill about 1 cm (½ in) deep and sow the seeds thinly.
- As they grow, you'll need to thin out the seedlings to keep them about 5 cm (2 in) apart or one per module if raised indoors. Discard the thinnings. ◀ 1
- When the plants are about 15 cm (6 in) tall, they are ready for transplantation to your chosen container. Choose the strongest seedlings.
- Using a dibber, make sufficiently deep holes for each seedling, and firm in using a tamper or your hand. In large containers, small plants should be spaced at a distance of about 25 to 30 cm (10 to 12 in) apart, depending on variety. Water well and gently fix a cabbage disc on the stem (see step 2 on page 37). ◀ 2
- For ready-grown seedlings, plant singly or in large containers as above.

Maintenance

- Keep the containers weed-free with careful hoeing.
- If birds are a problem, erect some netting or other protection (see pages 16–7).
- Keep well watered, especially in dry weather. Applying a mulch will help.
- Try protecting with fleece if cabbage butterflies are a problem; also, protect from strong sunlight as this causes the leaves to wilt.
- Feed with a nitrogen-rich liquid feed mid season.
- Remove any yellowing or damaged leaves as the plants grow, in order to prevent attracting pests and diseases.

Possible problems

Flea beetle, club root and caterpillars (see pages 18–9).

Harvesting, storing and freezing

Cut the heads of early-maturing calabrese with about 2.5 cm (1 in) of stalk in mid to late summer when the flower buds are green and tightly closed. Once the main head is cut, side shoots may grow and more heads will form on some varieties. Cut heads before flowers begin to open.

Sprouting broccoli should be cut with 10 to 15 cm (4 to 6 in) of stem for cooking whole. The remaining plant should be cut back to just above a pair of side shoots to encourage fresh spears to grow. Freshly picked spears can be kept in water, like a bunch of flowers, in the fridge for 2 to 3 days.

For freezing, wash carefully in cold water, strip off any leaves and trim away or peel any coarseness on the stems. Cut into florets. Blanch for 1 to 3 minutes, depending on thickness. Drain and cool, then open-freeze on trays before packing into freezer bags or rigid containers. Keep for up to 12 months. Cook from frozen in boiling water for 5 to 8 minutes.

Quick potted guide

CONTAINER Early maturing varieties are best suited for growing in pots with a minimum depth of 25 cm (10 in).

PLANT From seed in early to late spring. Buy seedlings for planting out in late spring.

POSITION Open position. Broccoli is perfectly hardy but calabrese is not frost-hardy. Both need protecting from excessive heat and strong sunlight.

SOIL Non-acid, fertile compost; good drainage.

HARVEST Mid to late summer.

▶ PRODUCE USED ON PAGES 108 & 116

Cabbage and Kale

(*Brassica oleracea* Capitata group)

(*Brassica oleracea* Alcephala group)

Quick potted guide

CONTAINER Compact varieties are best suited for growing in pots or window boxes with a minimum depth of 20 cm (8 in).

PLANT From seed in mid spring to early summer, depending on variety. Buy seedlings for planting out in late spring/summer.

POSITION Open position; cool or warmth; avoid excessive heat and strong sunlight.

SOIL Non-acid, fertile compost; good drainage.

HARVEST Midsummer to autumn, depending on variety.

The best cabbages and kales for container growing are compact, spring cabbages and dwarf varieties of kale. You'll get a quicker reward for your efforts, and tasty, lighter leaves for cooking with – excellent for steaming or stir-fries. However, if you do want to carry on growing throughout the colder months of the year, then winter cabbages in larger containers might be worth considering. Kale is the hardiest of all brassicas and the flavour is believed to be better after exposure to a frost.

Planting and siting

- The method for growing most types of cabbage and kale is very similar, but the timing varies according to variety. If planting from seed, both can be sown directly into outside containers. You will need two containers. If you have indoor space, seeds can be raised in modules until big enough to plant out.
- Make sure the compost is rich and fertile, and warmth will help the seeds germinate. Firm gently and make a drill about 1 cm (½ in) deep and sow the seeds thinly.
- As they grow, you'll need to thin out the seedlings to keep them about 5 cm (2 in) apart or one per module. Discard the thinnings. ▶ 1
- When the plants are 12 cm (5 in) tall, they are ready for transplantation into your chosen container. Choose the strongest seedlings.
- Using a dibber, make sufficiently deep holes for each seedling, and firm

in carefully using a tamper or your hand. In large containers, small plants should be spaced at a distance of about 25 to 45 cm (10 to 18 in) apart, depending on variety. Water well and gently fix a cabbage disc to the stems. ▶ **2**

- For ready-grown seedlings, plant singly or in large containers as above.

Maintenance

- Keep the containers weed-free.
- If birds are a problem, erect some netting or other protection (see pages 16–7).
- Water young plants in dry weather and keep watering until the plants are established. Water steadily especially kale, to avoid halting growth.
- Feed with a nitrogen-rich liquid feed mid season.
- Tie up large cabbage leaves with raffia or light string in summer if they start to loosen.
- Try protecting with fleece if cabbage butterflies are a problem. Also protect from strong sunlight as this causes the leaves to wilt.
- Remove any yellowing or damaged leaves as the plants grow in order to prevent attracting pests and disease.

Possible problems

Club root is the most serious cabbage disease but also cabbage root fly, caterpillars, and flea beetles. Kale is relatively trouble-free but slugs and snails love all cabbages and kale (see pages 18–9).

Harvesting, storing and freezing

Cut cabbages when the hearts are firm. ▶ **3** Use a knife to cut through the stem, just below the head and inside the loose leaves. In most cases, cabbages are cut for immediate use, but will keep for four to five days in the fridge. Remove the coarse outer leaves from a cabbage, then cut into quarters and slice out the hard central core and base stump. Wash thoroughly and drain, shaking to remove excess water. Kale is best picked as required. If caterpillars are a problem, soak the leaves in salted water to draw them off the plants before you prepare the leaves.

Freeze only young, crisp cabbage for best results. Trim away stalks and shred leaves, then blanch for 1 minute. Drain well and cool. Pack into freezer bags and use within six months. Cook from frozen in boiling water for 7 to 8 minutes. Kale is best frozen finely chopped as for cabbage, and used from frozen, added directly to soups and stews.

▶ PRODUCE USED ON PAGE 108

Cauliflower

(*Brassica oleracea* Botrytis group)

In the traditional garden setting, growing cauliflower is considered a bit of a challenge compared to other members of the Brassica family, but the rewards are great. New hybrids have been developed to produce less temperamental varieties, but good compost preparation and constant watering is essential for a good crop. Cauliflowers can be classified into the seasons they ripen; whilst the flavour is pretty much the same, the colour of the curd can be from bright white to cream, purple, green and even orange. Look for dwarf varieties and ones that have been developed specifically for container growing for best results – the foliage on dwarf varieties is still very bushy and you'll end up with lots of greenery which can take up quite a bit of space but it can be trimmed and eaten like greens. Cauliflower is raised from seed or ready-grown seedlings.

Planting and siting

- The method for growing different varieties of cauliflower is the same, but the timing varies according to variety. If planting from seed, cauliflower can be sown directly into outside containers. You will need two containers. If you have indoor space, seeds can be raised in modules until big enough to plant out.
- Make sure the compost is rich and fertile, and warmth will help the seeds germinate. Firm gently and make a drill about 1 cm (½ in) deep and sow the seeds thinly.
- As they grow, you need to thin out the seedlings to keep them about 5 cm (2 in) apart or one per module. Discard the thinnings. ◀ 1
- About six weeks or so later, when the plants have five or six leaves, they are ready for transplantation. Choose the strongest seedlings.
- Using a dibber, make sufficiently deep holes for each seedling and firm in carefully using a tamper or your hand. In large containers, small plants should be spaced at a distance of 15 to 30 cm (6 to 12 in) apart, depending on variety. Water well and gently fix a cabbage disc to the stems (see page 37).
- For ready-grown seedlings, plant singly or in large containers as above.

Maintenance

- Keep the containers weed-free.
- If birds are a problem, erect some netting or other protection (see pages 16–7).
- Keep well watered especially in dry weather and apply a mulch if preferred. As winter approaches, 'earth up' the compost to protect the stems, and keep the compost firm if the stems become loosened by the wind.
- Feed with a nitrogen-rich liquid feed mid season.
- Remove any yellowing or damaged leaves as the plants grow in order to prevent attracting pests and disease.

- Try protecting with fleece if cabbage butterflies are a problem. Also protect from strong sunlight as this causes the leaves to wilt.
- Once the curds form, break the stems of some of the outer leaves and fold them over the curds to keep them from discolouring. ◀ 2

Possible problems

Flea beetle, club root, caterpillars (see pages 18–9).

Harvesting, storing and freezing

Cut cauliflower heads when they are compact and firm, and dome-shaped. If left too long, the curds begin to separate as the plant begins to flower. Cut through the stem with a sharp knife, but don't cut off all the leaves as they will help preserve the curd. Cut cauliflower florets do not keep well in the fridge, so they are best prepared and cooked as quickly as possible.

Freeze in the same way as broccoli and calabrese (see page 35) but put a good squeeze of lemon juice in the water to help keep pale cauliflower curds from discolouring.

▶ PRODUCE USED ON PAGE 122

Oriental greens

Chinese cabbage and Pak choi (Bok choi) (*Brassica oleracea* Capitata group)

Mizuna (*Brassica rapa* var. *nipposinica*) and Mustard greens (*Brassica juncea*)

You'll find a huge selection of interesting-tasting leaves that come under this umbrella group. They are perfect for cooler climates and will provide excellent greenery for cooking and eating when other leaves are scarce. Ideal for container growing and some, like mizuna, make good cut-and-come-again crops, so are excellent value too. Chinese cabbages are the biggest of the Oriental greens and take up the most space – they can be eaten raw or shredded and stir-fried. Pak choi are small, compact bunches of leaves with a thick yet soft white stalk; quick growing and ready to harvest in about three to four weeks. When small and immature they can be eaten raw in salads, but if left to mature they can be braised or stir-fried. Mizuna is a Japanese salad brassica with fine feathery dark green leaves used for garnishings or in salads. It has a mild mustardy flavour and will be ready for harvest from four to eight weeks after sowing. The older leaves are better steamed or stir-fried. The flowering stalks can be eaten as well, steamed, like broccoli. Mustard greens can be grown as a large cabbage or as a leafy seedling to give a mustardy flavour to a salad. All can be grown from seed or ready-raised seedlings.

Quick potted guide

CONTAINER Suitable for all containers with a minimum depth of 10 cm (4 in).

PLANT From seed in spring, late summer to early autumn (depending on variety). Plant ready-raised seedlings from spring onwards.

POSITION Cool or warmth; avoid excessive heat and strong sunlight.

SOIL Moisture-retentive, non-acid compost.

HARVEST Late summer, autumn, winter (depending on variety).

Planting and siting

- For Chinese cabbage, sow from seed in early spring directly into an outdoor container (ideal for raising in grow-bags), in drills about 2 cm (³/₄ in) deep, and cover with fine compost.
- When large enough to handle, thin out to 10 cm (4 in) apart. Discard the thinnings.
- After a few weeks, thin the seedlings again to about 25 cm (10 in) apart – you can use the established seedlings as spring greens – leaving the strongest specimens to grow on. ▶ 1
- For other leaves, sow every two weeks from April to September directly into outdoor containers for a continuous supply. If indoors or under glass, you can grow these greens all year round. Sow thinly as above.
- Leave other leaves unthinned for salad leaves or thin to 15 cm (6 in) or more for larger plants.
- Ready-raised seedlings are ideal for grow-bags as well as other containers. Plant as above.

Maintenance

- Keep them weed-free and watered well.
- Try protecting with fleece to shield from strong sunlight as this causes the leaves to wilt (see step 2 on page 71).
- Birds may be a problem, so erect some netting or other protection.
- Remove yellowing or weak leaves using scissors. ▶ 2
- As winter approaches, protect over-wintering varieties with cloches (these do not have to be so well watered).
- For Chinese leaves, tie up the leaves with raffia or light string in summer if they start to loosen.

Possible problems

Flea beetles and slugs may be a problem (see pages 18–9).

Harvesting, storing and freezing

All Oriental leaves are best picked and used as required. None of them keep well, although you can submerge them in a bowl of cold water in the fridge and keep for up to 24 hours if necessary. Either pick off individual leaves – this way the plants will shoot up again – or pull up the whole plant. Oriental greens are not suitable for freezing unless part of a cooked dish. ▶ 3

▶ PRODUCE USED ON PAGES 106, 108 & 117

Spinach

(*Spinacia oleracea*)

including Chard (*Beta vulgaris* Cicla group)

Spinach is a plant for cool climates and doesn't like hot, dry weather. It is important to keep the crop watered, and you'll need to sow several batches to get a good yield. Sow and pick early for salad leaves, or leave longer for cooking. If you sow batches successively, you should get a good, long supply. Chard is easier to grow and is a great value crop. If you sow chard in the spring, you'll be able to enjoy the leaves in mid to late summer, and keep going right through until the following year as it over-winters well. Chard has a number of names such as Swiss, ruby or silver chard, and silver beet. The leaves and stalks are succulent and with so many varieties to choose from, you'll be able to create a truly multicoloured display. The bright colours do dull down on cooking, but like spinach, small young leaves make tasty raw salad leaves and garnishes. Both are usually grown from seed.

Planting and siting

- Spinach seeds are best sown directly into an outdoor container; spinach can also be grown as a 'fill-in' crop in between other vegetables, as they will shield the leaves from any harsh sunlight. Lightly firm the top of a container of compost. Sow the seeds liberally, but not too thickly, across the top of the container and cover with a light layer of compost. ◀ 1
- As they grow, you'll only need to thin out the seedlings if you want larger leaves; simply cut when required.
- Chard seeds can be sown directly into the container outside. For large leaves, make a drill about 1 cm (½ in) deep in the compost and sow the seeds thinly. For a salad crop, sow like spinach seed.
- As they grow, you'll need to thin out the seedlings when they are large enough to handle (about 10 cm / 4 in tall) – use the thinnings in salads. Water the day before to make thinning easier. Thin to stations about 20 cm (8 in) apart for larger leaves, less for smaller varieties.

Maintenance

- Keep weed-free and well watered. Do not let the compost dry as this may cause bolting.
- Try protecting spinach with fleece to shield it from strong sunlight as this causes the leaves to wilt (see step 2 on page 71).
- Birds may be a problem, so erect some netting or put in other protection (see pages 16–7).
- As winter approaches, protect over-wintering varieties with cloches (these do not have to be so well watered).

Possible problems

Can be susceptible to slugs and snail damage; also downy mildew (see pages 18–9).

Harvesting, storing and freezing

Pick young leaves of both plants to eat raw, or leave longer for cooking. Pick a few outside leaves before they become tough but avoid taking more than half of the plant otherwise it will be unable to regenerate. Leaves wilt quickly, so pick to order, rinse in water and use straight away. Leaves can be kept submerged in water in the fridge for 24 hours if necessary. ◀ 2

For freezing, choose young leaves and rinse well. Blanch in small quantities for 1 minute. Drain well and press out excess water. Allow to cool. Pack into rigid containers or freezer bags. Seal and store for up to 12 months. Cook from frozen with a small amount of water. Cover and cook for about 5 minutes, stirring occasionally to break up. Drain well and serve with butter.

Quick potted guide

CONTAINER Suitable for all containers with a minimum depth of 20 cm (8 in).

PLANT From seed in mid to late spring (spinach) and midsummer (chard).

POSITION Cool, open site; avoid heat and strong sunlight (spinach); open position; sun or light shade (chard).

SOIL Moist, non-acid, fertile compost.

HARVEST Early to late summer or winter, depending on variety.

▶ PRODUCE USED ON PAGE 121

Broad bean

(Fava bean)

(*Vicia faba*)

The most hardy of all beans, the broad bean is one of the best of home-grown vegetables as its taste is second to none when freshly picked. As well as the beans themselves, young beans can be cooked and eaten in the pod, and the shooting tops of the plants cook up like spinach and have an earthy/beany flavour. For container growing, choose dwarf varieties which grow between 30 to 45 cm (12 to 18 in) tall. The bean flowers are attractive and very fragrant, and the foliage will add a splash of bright green colour to your growing area. Broad beans are usually grown from seed but you can purchase seedlings from nurseries and garden centres in the spring.

Quick potted guide

CONTAINER Dwarf varieties are best suited for growing in pots with a minimum depth of 20 cm (8 in).

PLANT From seed in February to June, and October to November. Buy seedlings for planting out in late spring.

POSITION Open position.

SOIL Fertile, non-acid, moisture-retaining compost.

HARVEST Early to late summer, depending on variety.

Planting and siting

- If growing from seed, sow indoors, one bean per individual module (see page 14) for later potting on or transplanting. ▶ 1
- Once the seedlings are large enough to handle, in late spring, gradually accustom them to outside conditions, avoiding frosts, for a few days. After they have acclimatized, carefully transfer to an outside container of compost, spaced about 25 cm (10 in) apart to grow fully. ▶ 2
- Alternatively, sow beans directly into the container about 5 cm (2 in) deep. Take care not to overcrowd the container as broad beans like space as well as fertile compost. Plant seeds about 25 cm (10 in) apart.
- Water well after sowing and planting.
- For taller varieties, or if the growing area is windy, tie the stems to stakes or canes to secure them as they grow.

Maintenance

- When the first pods are about 10 cm (4 in) long, pinch out the growing tips to encourage an early crop to reduce the chance of blackfly (see page 18). ▶ 3
- Keep the weeds down and water during dry periods.

Possible problems

Broad beans are relatively trouble-free, apart from blackfly (see page 18).

Harvesting, storing and freezing

The earliest crops are ready in May. You can start to pick them when the pods are no more than 5 cm (2 in) long and cook them whole. Otherwise, pick the beans as required, feeling the pods to get an idea of the size of the beans within – ideally, the bean should not get beyond 2 cm (¾ in) diameter for the best flavour and texture. Once picked, the beans will keep in the fridge, unshelled, for two to three days.

For freezing, shell and, depending on the size of the bean, blanch for 1 to 2 minutes. Drain and cool before packing into freezer bags or rigid containers. Keep for up to 12 months. Cook from frozen in boiling salted water for 5 to 8 minutes.

▶ PRODUCE USED ON PAGE 112

French bean

(Green bean)

Phaseolus vulgaris

Quick potted guide

CONTAINER Dwarf varieties are best suited for growing in pots with a minimum depth of 20 cm (8 in).

PLANT From seed in April to June. Buy seedlings for planting out in late spring.

POSITION Sensitive to cold so shelter and warmth are preferable.

SOIL Fertile, non-acid compost; good drainage.

HARVEST Late summer to early autumn, before the first frosts.

In spite of their name, it appears that the beans originated from Peru, although they have long been loved in France. They love warmth and flourish in hot conditions. Unable to tolerate frosts, these beans should be planted out from late May onwards, but other than this, French beans are generally trouble- and disease-free. You'll find dwarf types ideal for container growing which require little support – taller varieties require the same support systems as runner beans. French beans are easy to pick, crisp in texture and full of flavour. They are usually grown from seed but you can purchase seedlings from nurseries and garden centres in the spring. Look out for disease-resistant varieties.

Planting and siting

- If growing from seed, sow indoors, one bean per individual module (see page 14) for later potting on or transplanting. Keep the compost moist at all times. French beans are more susceptible to the cold than broad beans so keep indoors to avoid being affected by the cold. ▶ 1
- Once the seedlings are large enough to handle, in late spring, gradually accustom them to outside conditions, avoiding frosts, for a few days. After they have acclimatized, carefully transfer to an outside container of compost, spaced about 20 cm (8 in) apart for dwarf varieties or further apart if larger. ▶ 2
- Alternatively, after risk of frost is over, sow beans directly into the container about 5 cm (2 in) deep. Plant seeds about 20 cm (8 in) apart.
- Water well after sowing and planting, but avoid over-watering and soaking the compost.
- Tie the stems to stakes or canes to secure them as they grow.

Maintenance

- Keep weeds down and water well, particularly in dry spells.

Possible problems

Slugs and snails are attracted to young foliage and pods. Blackfly and fungal diseases may also be a possibility (see pages 18–9).

Harvesting, storing and freezing

The plants will start to crop within eight weeks of sowing, and may produce pods for a couple of months afterwards. The more beans you pick, the more they will produce. Pick the young beans carefully to avoid pulling out the whole plant. Hold the stem with one hand and pull the pod downwards with the other. Young beans wither quite quickly after picking so they should be cooked or preserved as soon as possible. However, you can keep them wrapped in damp paper in the fridge overnight if you don't have the time to freeze them. ▶ 3

Young French beans are best for freezing. Top and tail. Leave small beans whole; larger ones are best cut into 2.5 to 5 cm (1 to 2 in) lengths. Blanch for 1 to 2 minutes. Drain and cool before packing into freezer bags or rigid containers. Keep for up to 12 months. Cook from frozen for about 5 minutes.

▶ PRODUCE USED ON PAGE 112

Pea

(Pisum sativum)

Of all the members of the legume family, peas are considered to be quite a difficult crop to grow, and they can take up a lot of space. Yet, dwarf varieties make an attractive crop and are much more low maintenance when grown in a container; above all else, the fresh produce is so rewarding it'll be well worth any effort. As well as the traditional round garden pea, you'll find tiny petit pois, flat-podded mangetout peas, and sweet and crisp sugarsnaps, all suitable for container growing. Young pea shoots can be snipped off and eaten as a delicious salad leaf with a distinct pea flavour. Look out for disease-resistant varieties, and remember to water well at the flowering stage to improve the crop. Peas can be planted from seed straight into the ground or from seedlings raised in the nursery or garden centre.

Planting and siting

- Peas are usually grown from seed, straight in the container, in mid spring. Do not add fertilizer at the time of sowing as this may cause the peas to grow too quickly and not form properly – use only a light dressing just before sowing.
- Choose a sunny spot to position your container and, using a dibber, make holes about 5 cm (2 in) deep, depending on the size and shape of your container, and sow the seeds about 15 cm (6 in) apart. Crops can be planted successively until early summer. ◀ **1**
- Supports such as thin twiggy sticks, canes or pea netting should be added to the container once the peas produce tendrils and start needing to climb. Seedlings should be planted out in late spring along with a support system. ◀ **2**

Maintenance

- Keep the container weed-free.
- Cover the newly sown seeds with netting to protect from birds and keep covered until the plants mature.
- Water during dry spells, especially once the flowers form. Applying a mulch can help conserve moisture during excessively dry weather.

Possible problems

Peas are prone to several pests and diseases. Slugs, birds and mice will eat the seeds and seedlings. Also susceptible to aphids, pea thrips and downy mildew (see pages 18–9).

Harvesting, storing and freezing

When the pods seem to have reached the right length, check them daily to feel if the peas are swelling inside. Aim to pick them when well developed

but not overly large. For all varieties, carefully pull the pod upwards with one hand whilst holding the stem with the other. Mangetout peas and sugarsnaps are ready to be picked when you can just see the peas forming in the pod – if you don't catch them at the right time, they will go on to develop into a garden pea and can be harvested and used as such. If insufficient mangetouts or sugarsnaps are ready at one time, pick the few that are ripe and keep in the fridge for a few days until others are ready for harvesting. Pick garden peas regularly and eat as fresh as possible.

For freezing, garden peas should be shelled, blanched for 1 minute, drained, cooled quickly in cold running water or iced water, dried and then packed into freezer bags. Top and tail mangetouts and sugarsnaps, blanch whole for 2 minutes, then cool and pack as for peas. Freeze for up to 12 months. Cook from frozen for 5 to 7 minutes.

▶ PRODUCE USED ON PAGES 108 & 111

Runner bean

(String bean)

Phaseolus coccineus

Runner beans are a true symbol of summer and a real favourite. Originating from Mexico, they are larger and coarser than the French variety but have much more flavour and a juicier texture than any other bean. The plant is attractive with striking scarlet or white flowers and vine-like greenery which traditionally grows up wigwam-shaped canes. You will find dwarf varieties as well as the traditional climbers; choose a variety akin to your space. Runner beans aren't able to tolerate frosts so should be planted out when there is no danger of extremely cold weather or frost. They also dislike very hot conditions (above 30°C/86°F) so should be sheltered. Runner beans are usually grown from seed but you can purchase seedlings from nurseries and garden centres in the spring.

Planting and siting

- If growing from seed, sow indoors, one bean per individual module or pot (see page 14) for later potting on or transplanting. Keep the compost moist at all times. Runner beans are more susceptible to the cold than broad beans so keep indoors to avoid being affected by the cold. ▶ 1
- Once the seedlings are large enough to handle, in late spring, gradually accustom them to outside conditions, avoiding frosts, for a few days.

Quick potted guide

CONTAINER Dwarf varieties are best suited for growing in pots with a minimum depth of 20 cm (8 in).

PLANT From seed in April to June. Buy seedlings for planting out in late spring.

POSITION Sun-loving but sensitive to extremes of temperature so appropriate protection is required.

SOIL Fertile, non-acid compost; good drainage.

HARVEST Midsummer to autumn, before the first frosts.

- Before transplanting traditional climbing beans, you'll need to erect some supports. You can train them to climb up a wigwam of about five tall canes tied at the top or buy a specialist frame to suit your container. The distance between canes should be about 20 cm (8 in) for easier picking. ▶ **2**
- After they have acclimatized, carefully transfer to the outside container and plant one per cane or support stick.
- Alternatively, after risk of frost is over, sow beans directly into a container with a support structure as described above, about 5 cm (2 in) deep, one seed per cane.
- Water well after sowing and planting.

Maintenance

- Encourage young seedlings to climb up the canes until they get established.
- Once the plants have reached the top of the canes, remove the growing tops. For dwarf varieties, pinch out any long shoots. ▶ **3**
- Keep weeds down and keep watered to prevent drying out, especially after the flowers appear. Mist the flowers with tepid water to encourage the beans to set.

Possible problems

Slugs and snails, blackfly or powdery mildew (see pages 18–9).

Harvesting, storing and freezing

Pick the beans while they are slender and young, before the seeds begin to swell in the pods. The more they are picked, the more they will produce. For this reason, large oversized beans are better removed to encourage new growth – the larger and older the bean, the tougher and more tasteless it will become. Once the beans are picked, any that can't be used straightaway can be stored in a jug of water, stem end in the water, in the fridge for two to three days.

For freezing, wash the beans well when ready to cook them. Cut off the tops and tails and trim away any stringy edges. If you have a specialist bean shredder, you'll be able to cut the beans into long, thin shreds, otherwise cut into diagonal slices if you want a firmer texture. Blanch for 2 minutes, then drain and cool before packing into freezer bags or rigid containers. Keep for up to 12 months. Cook from frozen for about 5 minutes.

▶ PRODUCE USED ON PAGE 112

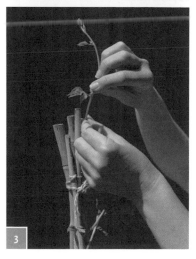

Aubergine
(Eggplant)

(Solanum melongena)

Originating from Asia, this attractive tropical plant with exotic-looking shiny fruit of black, purple, pink or white belongs to the same family as the potato and is related to the tomato. Aubergines can be grown in the same way as tomatoes but they are much more sensitive to the cold and are slower to grow. They need steady warmth and sunshine to ripen properly, and can grow outside in a warm, sunny, sheltered position, but must be started off indoors in order to germinate and develop properly. Choose a dwarf variety for growing in small pots on a windowsill.

Planting and siting

- If growing from seed, soak in water overnight before sowing as thinly as possible in individual modules or pots as described on page 14. In order to germinate, the temperature needs to be between 20–25°C (68–77°F), so keep indoors in warm conditions and cover with a propagation lid. ▶ 1 & 2

Quick potted guide

CONTAINER Most varieties are suitable for grow-bags and pots with a minimum depth of 15 cm (6 in); dwarf varieties can be grown in window boxes.

PLANT From seed in spring or buy seedlings in late spring/early summer.

POSITION Warm, sunny and sheltered.

SOIL Rich, well-drained compost.

HARVEST Midsummer onwards

- Once seedlings are large enough to handle, carefully thin out to leave the strongest specimens. Discard the thinnings.
- In early summer, once the seedlings are about 30 cm (12 in) high, carefully transfer to grow-bags (two or three per bag, depending on the size of the bag and aubergine variety) or other containers of choice.
- Tie the stem to a cane for support, and water well. Only put outside when the temperature is a guaranteed 15°C (59°F) or above, otherwise keep indoors in a sunny porch, conservatory or windowsill. ▶ 3

Maintenance

- Keep well watered and weed-free.
- Mist frequently to keep down the risk of pests, and to help fertilize the flowers when they form.
- Feed every 10 days to two weeks with a high-potash liquid feed once the fruit has started to develop.
- When five fruits have developed, remove lateral shoots and any other flowers that form in order to help the fruit develop.

Possible problems

Red spider mite, aphids and whitefly (see pages 18–9).

Harvesting, storing and freezing

Aubergines are ready for picking when the overall colour is evenly distributed, usually between July and October. Handle the fruits carefully to avoid damaging and bruising them, and use scissors to snip them from the stalks. Once picked, aubergines in perfect condition will keep in the refrigerator for about a week.

Wipe aubergines with a damp cloth and trim off the stalks before cooking or freezing. Only freeze aubergine fruit if in tip top condition. Slice or dice, and then 'salt' by placing in a colander or large sieve set over a bowl and sprinkle evenly with salt. Leave to drain for 30 to 40 minutes and no longer than 1 hour, then rinse thoroughly (salting helps tenderize the flesh during cooking – unsalted aubergines tend to have a spongier texture when cooked). Blanch for 2 minutes, then rinse in cold water, dry and cool. Open-freeze and pack into freezer bags or rigid containers. Store for up to 12 months. Frozen aubergine is only suitable for soups, stews or baked dishes because it becomes very soft once thawed; therefore it is best used directly from frozen in your chosen recipe.

▶ PRODUCE USED ON PAGE 120

1

2

3

Courgette
(Zucchini)
and Summer squash

(*Cucurbita pepo*)

Quick potted guide

CONTAINER Suitable for all containers with a minimum depth of 25 cm (10 in).

PLANT From seed in late spring/early summer. Buy seedlings for planting out in late spring/summer.

POSITION Sheltered position; sun-loving; frost-intolerant.

SOIL Rich, fertile compost.

HARVEST Midsummer onwards, depending on variety.

Of all members of the cucurbit family, courgettes and smaller varieties of summer squash are best suited to container growing – marrows, pumpkin and winter squash tend to take up too much space in a small area. You'll find plenty of shapes and sizes to choose from, but in the kitchen, they are all used in the same way, so choose a variety to suit your space and requirements. Courgettes and summer squash grow best in larger containers; they can be trained over trellis, and have large, spreading or trailing foliage and big yellow flowers. These plants are half-hardy and need sunshine and shelter, a good supply of water and nutrients. You can grow both from seed or you will find ready-sprouted seedlings in the nursery or garden centre.

Planting and siting

- For sowing from seed indoors, soak the seeds overnight to speed up germination. Plants can be raised indoors, in modules in late spring (see page 14). Cover with a propagation lid for best results. ▶ 1
- For sowing directly into the container outside, wait until the danger of frost has passed. Make a hole about 2.5 cm (1 in) deep and plant three

seeds close together. Cover with compost and then cover with a small cloche on top until the seeds have germinated. ▶ 2

- After germination, when the first true leaves have formed, thin out the weakest seedlings to leave the strongest to develop. Allow 60 cm (24 in) or more between seedlings if planting in large containers. Scatter slug pellets, or similar deterrent, around. ▶ 3

Maintenance

- Keep weeded and water generously around the seedlings, not on them.
- Keep slugs at bay by renewing pellets or other deterrent.
- Bush types can be allowed to spread themselves, while trailing varieties may need trimming if they begin to sprawl and take over, or training into shape over trellis or frames.
- Once the fruits start to swell, feed with a tomato fertilizer every two weeks. Rest larger squash on upturned terracotta plant saucers or ceramic tiles to prevent them rotting and being attacked by slugs.

Possible problems

Generally trouble-free. Can be prone to slug damage, and cucumber mosaic virus is the most common disease (see pages 18–9).

Harvesting, storing and freezing

Courgettes and summer squash are delicate in flavour and are best eaten fresh – they are very watery and soon dehydrate, so don't store well. Harvest by cutting the fruit off the stalks about 2 cm (3/4 in) away from the fruit using a sharp knife. For courgettes, cut when the fruits are still young or about 10 cm (4 in) long. They are best cut and used straight away although they will keep for three to four days in the fridge. Summer squash should be ready for picking in July – look for the stem beginning to split as an indicator that they are ready to pick. The skin should be soft enough to be able to pierce easily with a round bladed knife.

Choose only firm and young produce for freezing. Wash, trim and cut into pieces about 1 cm (1/2 in) thick or leave whole. Blanch for 1 minute, drain, cool and pack in rigid containers between sheets of freezing paper. Keep for up to one year. Partially thaw and then fry in hot oil or butter for 2 to 3 minutes on each side. Alternatively, cook the slices in butter before freezing, then thaw completely before reheating in a frying pan for 3 to 4 minutes until piping hot.

▶ PRODUCE USED ON PAGES 107, 108, 116 & 134

Mushroom

(Agaricus)

This versatile kitchen ingredient is one of the few home-grown vegetables you can grow and enjoy all year round without even going outside. You just need to make sure you get your preparation right and then maintain your crop, as you would any other. You'll find specialized mushroom growing kits in most garden centres or specialist retailers, offering mushroom-impregnated compost with varieties such as shiitake, chestnut, button or oyster. There are also impregnated logs for putting outside. The most cost-effective way is to buy some dry spawn in packets, available from seed merchants, and either follow the manufacturer's instructions or the steps below.

Planting and siting

- Fill your chosen container with moist, very fertile compost or well-rotted manure, and press down well.
- Scatter the dry spawn evenly over the surface and then mix into the top 5 cm (2 in) of compost. ◀ 1
- Cover completely with damp newspaper. Store in a cool place (darkness is not essential) at around 15°C (59°F). After a few days, the spawn will start to 'run', and thin white fungal threads (mycelium) will form on the surface; this is the first stage of mushroom formation. ◀ 2
- About two weeks after the mycelium forms, remove the newspaper and cover the top with a 'casing' of about 2.5 cm (1 in) moist compost.

Maintenance

- Throughout the growing period, keep the surface of the compost moist but not soaking – you may find a mister useful for this.
- Keep the mushroom container shielded from sunlight and at a steady temperature as fluctuations in temperature will inhibit growth.
- Pick off any damaged, old or diseased mushrooms.

Possible problems

Temperature is the main problem when growing mushrooms – temperatures below 10°C (50°F) and above 20°C (68°F) will not suit the growing spawn. Take care not to over-water as this will rot the fungus.

Harvesting, storing and freezing

Mushrooms grow in batches, so you might end up with lots together and then go through a barren period when not much is produced. If the conditions are right, you should be able to harvest mushrooms up to six months from spawning. To pick, gently twist the mushroom by its cap and pull it away from the bed without damaging any of the surrounding

Quick potted guide

CONTAINER Approximately 25 g (1 oz) dry spawn will be sufficient to cover an area about 30 cm (12 in) square and 18 cm (7 in) deep.

PLANT From dry spawn all year round.

POSITION Cool storage area such as a cupboard or shed; ideal temperature 15°C (59°F).

SOIL Very fertile compost or very well rotted manure.

HARVEST All year round: 10 to 12 weeks in ideal conditions.

mushrooms or disturbing the growing bed. The more you pick the more will form. Mushrooms dehydrate quickly once they are picked but if you need to keep them, do not wash them, just wipe off any compost and either keep them on kitchen paper in open trays or pack them loosely in paper bags and store for two to three days in the fridge.

Mushrooms are best cooked before freezing as they go very slimy once thawed. Either incorporate them as part of a recipe, or wipe, slice and fry them in a little butter and oil for 2 to 3 minutes. Cool and drain well, then pack into freezer bags or rigid containers and store for up to six months. They are best reheated from frozen or added straight into soups and stews as needed.

▶ PRODUCE USED ON PAGES 110 & 116

Pepper and Chilli

(*Capsicum* species)

Quick potted guide

CONTAINER Suitable for all containers with a minimum depth of 20 cm (8 in).

PLANT From seed in spring. Buy seedlings for planting out in late spring.

POSITION Warm, sunny site (peppers and chillies are not hardy).

SOIL Very fertile compost.

HARVEST Midsummer onwards.

Usually associated with hothouse growing, there are varieties that will grow outside as long as it's sunny and warm. Ideally, all varieties thrive in a sunny site indoors – you'll find mini varieties perfect for growing on windowsills. Sweet pepper or capsicum, pimento and bell peppers are annuals and the easiest to grow. They come in all shapes and sizes and in a selection of colours from a creamy white, to green, yellow and orange, through to red and the darkest purple or black. Chillies are perennial and the fruits are smaller and again vary in colour; the fiery heat will depend on the variety – Jalapeños are one of the mildest, whilst Habanero are extraordinarily hot! Peppers and chillies can be grown from seed or ready-raised seedlings.

Planting and siting

- Indoors, sow the seeds as thinly as possible in individual modules or pots as described on page 14. In order to germinate, the temperature needs to be 18°C (65°F). Cover with a propagator lid for best results.
- Once seedlings are showing three leaves, carefully thin out to leave the strongest specimens. Discard the thinnings.

- Once the seedlings are about 7 cm (3 in) high, carefully transfer to slightly larger pots. ▶ **1**
- Once they reach about 18 cm (7 in) repot into their final container, about 22 cm (9 in) deep or three per grow-bag. It is beneficial to restrict the growth of peppers and chillies slightly as this will encourage the plants to fruit.
- Only put outside if the temperature is a guaranteed 15°C (59°F) or above, otherwise keep indoors in a sunny porch, conservatory or windowsill.

Maintenance

- Keep containers weed-free.
- Mist frequently to keep down the risk of an attack by red spider mites. ▶ **2**
- Water peppers well but take care not to sodden the compost.
- Feed every 10 days with a high potash feed once the fruit develops. Take care not to over-water chillies, but ensure they are well fed.
- For taller varieties, tie the stems to canes for support. ▶ **3**

Possible problems

Red spider mite, aphids and whitefly (see pages 18–9).

Harvesting, storing and freezing

Green peppers should be ready to pick from midsummer onwards. Choose them when they are bright and shiny. Picking will encourage others to grow. If you want yellow or red, leave them on the plants to change colour if applicable to the variety, however, hot weather and sunshine are essential to ripen the peppers further. Peppers and chillies are best picked to use as soon as possible but will keep in the fridge for a couple days — chillies tend to go limp more quickly than peppers.

For freezing, prepare peppers by halving and removing the seeds and stalk. Either keep in halves, or slice or chop. Blanch for 1 to 3 minutes, depending on size, then drain, cool and pat dry. Pack into freezer bags and seal well. Keep for up to 12 months. Thaw halves of pepper for a couple of hours ready for using stuffed, or add sliced and chopped peppers directly to soups and stews, or other cooked dishes. If you want to freeze chillies, it is best to deseed and chop them first (they won't need blanching) and pack carefully in small bundles, well wrapped and easily identifiable. Store for up to six months and use straight from frozen.

▶ PRODUCE USED ON PAGES 106, 112, 116, 117 & 125

Sweetcorn

(*Zea mays*)

A tall bushy plant that wouldn't be your first thought for container growing, but if you have a sunny position and are looking for something dramatic to grow, sweetcorn is worth considering because the cobs are much more tasty than anything you can buy. You will find sweetcorn varieties that have been developed to cope with cooler climates and those that are better picked as baby corn. Sweetcorn is raised from seed or ready-grown seedlings.

Planting and siting

- In order to germinate, the temperature needs to be 18°C (65°F), so sow indoors. Sweetcorn doesn't like its roots disturbed, so ideally sow the seeds in individual biodegradable pots (see page 14). Cover with a propagator lid for best results. ◀ 1
- Once the seedlings have established you will need to repot them into larger biodegradable pots. ◀ 2
- When the risk of frost has passed and when the seedlings have five true leaves, they are ready to plant whole, with pot, in your prepared container of warm compost. ◀ 3
- Alternatively, when outside conditions are warm enough, sow two seeds about 2.5 cm (1 in) deep, directly into containers of warm compost. Lightly cover with compost and place a cloche or other protective covering on top.
- Once large enough to handle, remove the weaker seedling of the two and discard. Cloches and coverings can be removed once the seedlings have five true leaves.
- Ready-grown seedlings should be acclimatized once they have five true leaves before planting out into your container as above.

Maintenance

- Sweetcorn grows tall and is shallow-rooted so place in a sheltered position and weed carefully, taking extra care not to disturb the roots.
- Once established, growing plants may need earth drawn up around the base of the stems for stability, or require a support system such as a wigwam of canes (see Runner bean on pages 50–1).
- Sweetcorn is wind-pollinated so if your outdoor space is sheltered you may need to hand-pollinate by stroking the silky female tassels with pollen from the male flower that grows at the top.
- Water as required, especially in dry weather when the plants are flowering. Once the cobs start to swell, water with a liquid feed.

Possible problems

Apart from the elements, and mice and birds, sweetcorn is relatively trouble-free.

Harvesting, storing and freezing

Cobs are usually ready for picking about six weeks after the silvery silky tassels appear. The aim is to pick them before the sugar turns to starch to ensure they will be sweet and tender. The tassels will shrivel and turn brown as the seeds or kernels develop and change colour from light to deep yellow. Carefully pull back the covering leaves from the cob and gently press a fingernail into one of the kernels; if it exudes a milky liquid, the cobs should be picked and used, and if there is no liquid, the cob is well passed its prime. Either twist the cobs from the stalks or snap them off outwards. Use them quickly as they dry out fast and lose their flavour. Baby corn are ready about 16 weeks after planting and should be picked before they get too large, otherwise the central core becomes hard and inedible ▶ 4

Select young cobs and strip off the outer leaves. Blanch whole for about 3 minutes, then cool and dry. Either wrap whole and pack into containers or freezer bags. Alternatively, strip the kernels from the cobs using a sharp knife and blanch for about 1 minute. Baby corn should be blanched whole for 1 minute. Freeze for up to 12 months. Thaw whole cobs thoroughly before cooking for 6 to 7 minutes – don't add salt to the water as this will toughen them, but add 1 teaspoon of white sugar to sweeten them further. Kernels can be cooked from frozen for about 5 minutes, or added directly to soups and casseroles.

4

▶ PRODUCE USED ON PAGES 116 & 125

Herbs and edible flowers

If you like cooking, then you'll certainly want to make room for a pot or two of herbs. With pretty foliage and flowers, they're a good choice for brightening up a dull space, and some will even add a gentle wafting fragrance if you brush past them or rub their leaves. Herbs are very adaptable and will usually thrive wherever they are put, but ideally they like a sunny position, plenty of watering and well-drained compost. Some herbs like mint are invasive and will spread like wildfire, so plant them on their own. Choosing which ones to grow will depend on your culinary repertoire, but the following are the most commonly grown and used. Most herbs can be grown from seed or ready-raised seedlings.

Basil (*Ocimum basilicum*)

Bay (*Laurus nobilis*)

Calendula or Pot Marigold (*Calendula officinalis*)

Chervil (*Anthriscus cerefolium*)

Chives (*Allium schoenoprasum*)

Coriander (*Coriandrum sativum*)

Curry plant (*Helichrysum angustifolium*)

Dill (*Anethum graveolens*)

Lavender (*Lavendula augustifolia*)

Lemon balm (*Melissa officinalis*)

Marjoram (*Origanum vulgaris*)

Mint (*Mentha spitica*)

Nasturtium (*Tropaeolum majus*)

Pansy (*Viola x wikktrockiana*)

Parsley (*Petroselinum crispum*)

Rosemary (*Rosmarinus officinalis*)

Sage (*Salvia officinalis*)

Tarragon (*Artemisia dracunculsus*)

Thyme (*Thymus vulgaris*)

BASIL A staple herb for Italian cooking with a sweet peppery flavour and soft leaves that also make it a good addition to the salad bowl. Basil likes lots of sun and is perfect for a sunny windowsill in a pot with a minimum depth of 25 cm (10 in) and well-drained fertile compost. There are two varieties: sweet and bush. Neither is hardy and both require frequent watering. Basil is not suitable for freezing on its own; it is best added to other ingredients in a recipe. In late spring/early summer, you can put basil plants outside and, as basil attracts bees, it is a good idea to put a pot near plants that need pollinating.

BAY Sweet bay or bay laurel has aromatic leaves that can be used fresh or dried, in sweet or savoury dishes. Native to the Mediterranean region, it is pretty hardy when grown as a shrub but does require some protection from frosts and strong wind. Bay loves the sun. Plant in a large pot of fertile, well-drained compost, with a minimum depth of 20 to 30 cm (8 to 12 in), depending on the size of the plant, and prune any long or straggly branches to restrict growth and keep tidy. Once established, the evergreen leaves can be picked at any time of the year. Not suitable for freezing. ▶ 1

CALENDULA OR POT MARIGOLD Used by the Romans as we would use saffron, the fragrant orange and yellow petals of calendula are not only bright and cheerful but add a pleasant floweriness to salads. Calendulas don't like the cold and are not frost-hardy, so keep in the sun, in a container of fertile, free-draining compost, about 15 cm (6 in) deep. The petals are not suitable for freezing and lose their flavour when dried. ▶ 2

CHERVIL A hardy herb with fine, feathery leaves and a very mild, sweet aniseed flavour. Chervil is frost-hardy and likes free-draining compost in a container about 10 cm (4 in) deep. It prefers a partially shaded site. It is traditionally used with fish and chicken dishes, and makes a lovely flourishing garnish, or a salad ingredient. It can also be frozen (see page 67) for adding to soups, sauces and stocks. Not suitable for drying. ▶ 3

CHIVES Fine tubular leaves with a mild oniony flavour and lovely pink tufty flowers which make an eye-catching garnish and a tasty addition to salads. The herb is hardy and needs little attention, but will spread if not contained in small clumps. Prefers rich, moist, well-drained compost but will tolerate most soils in a container depth of about 18 cm (6 in). Chopped chives cook well and add an oniony flavour to savoury bakes and dishes. Cut chives as close to the ground as possible and cut each clump in turn to encourage new leaves to grow. Chives will freeze or dry (see page 67). ▶ 4

CORIANDER A hardy annual herb that can be grown for its leaves and seeds. Mature coriander plants produce small flower heads which form in clusters. After the flowers finish, the seed pods (or fruit) appear. These are

soft when they first form and need to dry out in the sun or indoors to form the spice seeds we are familiar with. As the fruits mature, they become spicy and emit an aroma that is a good indication they are ready for picking. The ferny leaves are sweet and delicately flavoured and are used in Indian, Middle Eastern and Oriental cooking, and also make a lovely salad leaf. The leaves can be frozen but do not dry very well (see page 67). Coriander does require sunshine but is otherwise easy to grow; plant in free-draining compost with a minimum depth of 7 cm (3 in) for best results. The seeds are ready for harvesting in late summer, and should be cut off at the seed head and either dried in the sun or indoors. The seeds can then be shaken out of the heads and stored in airtight containers for grinding and using in sweet and savoury cooking.

CURRY PLANT Intense silver, evergreen foliage which smells deliciously of sweet Indian curry. It loves full sun and rich, well-drained compost in a container about 18 cm (6 in) deep. Prune lightly in early autumn or spring. Protect in winter with a cloche or some garden fleece. Pick the leaves anytime for using in soups, stews, rice dishes and pickles. Remove sprigs before serving. Not suitable for freezing or drying.

DILL A semi-hardy annual herb with a mild aniseed flavour, traditionally used with fish. It will tolerate most well-drained soils in a container about 25 cm (10 in) deep, and loves the sun. The seeds can also be harvested for using during winter months. The fine feathery leaves will be ready for picking about eight weeks after sowing. They can be dried or frozen before the flowers form (see page 67). For seeds, leave the plants from the earliest sowing and pick the heads when they turn brown (usually in September). Treat as for coriander seeds (see above).

LAVENDER As well as emitting a heavenly fragrance, lavender is a useful herb to grow in a pot for culinary and household use. It also helps deter predating insects. Look for dwarf varieties for container growing. Lavender needs full sun with well-drained compost at a depth of about 20 cm (8 in). The flowers can be dried and used to flavour jams, white sugar, vinegars and salads. Dried flowers can also be bundled or put in sachets to scent clothes and protect linen from moths. Gather the flowers just before they open for best results. Not suitable for freezing. ▶ 4

LEMON BALM A lemon-scented hardy perennial, great for attracting bees. It is best contained as it can be invasive. Lemon balm isn't fussy about compost, and the minimum pot depth should be 20 cm (8 in). Prune regularly to maintain bushy growing habit. Use the leaves to make a refreshing 'tea', or for adding 'zing' to cold drinks and punches, to flavour white sugar, or for preserves, desserts and salads. Not suitable for freezing or drying.

Quick potted guide

CONTAINER Suitable for most containers with a minimum depth of 7 cm (3 in) to 30 cm (12 in), depending on variety.

PLANT From seed in late spring or buy seedlings for planting out in early summer, unless otherwise specified.

POSITION Warm, sunny, sheltered site (see individual entries for more specific information).

SOIL Well-drained compost.

HARVEST Spring to autumn, depending on variety.

MARJORAM Sweet marjoram has fine aromatic leaves and pink flowers which can be used to flavour a wide variety of dishes. The 'pot' dwarf variety is also half-hardy but the flavour is milder. All varieties prefer hot conditions, and the dwarf variety can easily be grown indoors for an all-year-round supply. Marjoram prefers free-draining compost and a depth of 10 cm (4 in) minimum. The soft leaves are widely used in Italian cookery, going especially well with tomatoes and fish. The leaves are ready for harvesting from May to September, and the tiny pink flowers from June onwards. The leaves will dry or freeze but for the best flavour should be picked for freezing before the plant starts flowering (see page 67).

MINT There are many different varieties you can grow, such as apple, pineapple, ginger, spearmint and peppermint. Leaves vary in flavour, size, colour and texture, so the choice is a personal one, but spearmint and apple mint are good choices for most cooks. Mint flowers grow in conical clusters of tiny pink, mauve or white petals, and make pretty garnishes. All mints are invasive and can easily take over a mixed container if not restricted. They are frost-hardy and prefer damp conditions in moisture-retaining compost about 15 cm (6 in) deep. Traditionally made into a sauce to serve with roast lamb, the leaves are often used as garnishes and as a flavouring for cooking vegetables such as peas and new potatoes. Pick fresh green leaves in May until early autumn. Mint will dry or freeze for winter use (see page 67). ▶ 4

NASTURTIUM These are attractive plants that offer a riot of colour. They are easy to grow from seed with edible flowers, leaves and seeds, all tasting mildly peppery. Frost-tender, nasturtiums like the sunshine, and like poor compost at a depth of about 15 cm (6 in). Slugs love them too! Flowers and leaves can be added to salads or sandwiches, and the seeds can be pickled like capers. Not suitable for freezing or drying. ▶ 5

PANSY A dainty splash of colour in spring and autumn, pansies prefer cool weather and wilt quickly in the heat. They like moist, fertile compost at a depth of 10 cm (4 in) minimum. The petals are mild and sweet and look lovely in salads or as a decoration for sweet dishes. Not suitable for freezing or drying.

PARSLEY Widely used as a garnish or 'chopping' herb for sauces, stuffings and salads. Parsley is best grown as an annual, and to ensure a constant supply, make two sowings: in March for summer and autumn, and again in July for winter and spring. Choose rich, free-draining compost in a container about 20 cm (8 in) deep. Flat-leaved varieties make for a better garnish, but the curly leaf varieties have more flavour. Cut one or two sprigs at a time from each plant until well established and remove any stems that are going to seed as this will encourage new growth. From June, sprigs can be dried or frozen (see page 67).

ROSEMARY A hardy evergreen shrub synonymous with the Mediterranean where it is used both in the kitchen and in medicine. The coarse leaves have a sweet resinous quality which goes well with lamb, game and other meat. Its woody stems make it ideal for pushing into meats and vegetables to flavour during slow cooking. The herb flowers can be white, pale blue or lilac and make a fragrant garnish. Rosemary needs sunshine, a well-drained compost, and protection from cold wind. The minimum container depth should be 20 cm (8 in). It requires frequent pruning to keep it in shape and is best propagated from cuttings or from a nursery-raised plant. Pick young leaves and stems for immediate use, although they will keep fresh for a couple of days in a jug of water. The leaves dry and freeze well (see page 67).

SAGE A downy soft, grey-green-leaved herb, but purple and variegated varieties are also available. A rich flavoured herb that is usually mixed with onion to accompany pork, goose and other rich meats. Pretty pink sage flowers can be added to salads or used as a floating garnish for soups. A hardy, evergreen herb that likes free-draining compost at a minimum depth of 20 cm (8 in). It can be harvested all year round, but the best-flavoured leaves are just before the herb flowers. The leaves wilt soon after picking but will dry or freeze (see page 67). Best raised from nursery-grown seedlings.

TARRAGON Soft, pointed long leaves with a mild, sweet, slightly aniseed flavour, used with fish, chicken and vegetables. Prefers warmth and is not frost-hardy. Plant in rich, free-draining compost with a minimum depth of 25 cm (10 in). Tarragon is a staple of the French kitchen and is often used in the making of herb vinegars. It will grow easily with little attention. Pick leaves from June to September. Best eaten fresh.

THYME Culinary thyme is native to the Mediterranean. There are several varieties, but the common and lemon varieties are the most popular. Thyme is excellent for use in slow cooking and imbues dishes with a fragrant woodiness which goes well with mushrooms, tomatoes, rich meat, fish and chicken – small bunches can be laid on top of roasting foods to penetrate them with flavour during cooking. It is an evergreen hardy plant that grows well in the sun and any well-drained compost in a container depth of 15 cm (6 in). It is frost-hardy and drought resistant. Pick the sprigs when needed, and the flowers can be used as a garnish or added to salads. Prune after flowering to retain bushy growing habit. It freezes and dries well (see page 67).

Possible problems

Slugs, snails, birds and mice (see pages 18–9).

Harvesting, storing and freezing herbs

Use scissors to cut fresh herbs, and because most herbs and flowers wilt soon after harvesting, use as soon as possible. Placing them in water like a bunch of flowers will keep them for an extra hour or so, but for keeping for a couple of days, rinse them in water, shake dry and put in a large plastic food bag with air, seal tightly and store in the bottom of the fridge. If you have space, submerging them in a bowl of cold water in the fridge will also keep them fresh for a few days though you'll need to change the water every day. ▶ **6 & 7**

Herbs have a freezer life of about six months, after which time the flavour is lost. They are unsuitable for garnishes once thawed, but are fine for cooking used straight from frozen and can be crumbled directly into the cooking pot or mixture. Evergreen herbs are not worth freezing since it is always better to use fresh, and in general, freeze the herbs that you are most likely to use, e.g. chives, parsley, sage or dill. Pick fresh, wash, drain and pat dry. Keep different varieties separate from each other so that there is no transference of flavour. Herbs don't need blanching and they can either be frozen in sprigs, well-sealed in small freezer bags, or chopped and packed into ice cube trays: use 1 tablespoon of chopped herb with 1 tablespoon of water per cube and wrap the tray in cling film when frozen to help preserve the flavour; these can be added directly to recipes.

To dry herbs, pick when they are in peak condition, on a dry, warm day. It is best not to wash herbs before drying as they need to be as dry as possible. Simply shake lightly to remove any trapped compost if necessary. Choose a warm, dry, dark, well-ventilated place, ideally around 24–26° C (75–79° F); darkness helps prevent the herb oils from evaporating. Soft-leaved herbs should dry in four to five days, and up to two weeks for the coarser-textured herbs. Hang stems of the same variety in bunches of about 10 stems maximum tied with string, upside down, with the heads loosely packed in paper bags. Smaller quantities can be dried by spreading out on a tightly lined muslin frame, or brown paper punctured with fine holes spread on a wire rack. The herbs are ready when the leaves are paper-dry and fragile. Pack them in airtight containers without breaking them up too much in order to preserve their flavour. Dark glass containers are preferable for storage as plastic absorbs aromas and metal can affect the flavour. Always keep in a dark, dry place.

6

7

▶ PRODUCE USED THROUGHOUT BUT SPECIFICALLY ON PAGES 107, 122 & 127

Summer radish

(Raphanus sativus)

Summer radish is one of the prettiest, daintiest roots you can grow; they're also very tasty, and quick and easy to grow. Radishes were grown by the ancient Egyptians and were probably introduced to the UK by the Romans. Summer varieties are best for container growing as they mature quickly. These radishes include the familiar small, round, deep pink in colour favourites that have been gracing our salad bowl for years. All radishes have a crisp white flesh but the flavour varies between mild and strong mustard. Summer radishes are among some of the quickest-growing vegetables and can be grown all year round if protected from frosts by cloches, but they do like lots of water. They can be grown on their own or make a useful fill-in crop to grow in between slower-to-mature vegetables. Summer radishes are usually raised from seed.

Planting and siting

- Choose a sunny site for your summer radish container. Make a drill about 1 cm (½ in) deep and sow the fine seeds as thinly as possible so that little thinning is required.
- Sift a very thin covering of compost over the top and water well. Leave about 15 cm (6 in) between rows. It is worth considering that once summer radishes are mature they should be pulled as their texture declines rapidly; it is probably better to sow successively in two-week intervals rather than planting several rows at the same time. ◀ 1
- When the radish shoots are big enough to handle, thin to about 2.5 to 5 cm (1 to 2 in) apart, depending on the expected radish size. Discard the thinnings.

Maintenance

- Keep the pot weed-free using a small garden hand fork or an old kitchen fork to prevent damage to the roots. ◀ 2
- Continue to water radish crops throughout the summer to prevent them drying out, as lack of water will inhibit growth.
- If birds are a problem, you may need to protect the crop with netting or other protection.

Possible problems

Although classified as a root vegetable, radishes are related to brassicas and succumb to the same pests (see pages 36–7).

Harvesting, storing and freezing

From four to six weeks after sowing, summer radishes will be ready for pulling. Pull as many as are needed when they are young and tender.

If necessary, keep in a jug of water in the fridge, like a bunch of flowers, for two to three days. Trim away leaves and root ends and wash well before serving. Radishes are not suitable for freezing.

Quick potted guide

CONTAINER Suitable for all containers and window boxes with a minimum depth of 10 cm (4 in).

PLANT Early spring onwards.

POSITION Open, sunny site.

SOIL Light, free-draining compost.

HARVEST Late spring onwards.

Lettuce

(Lactuca sativa)

When it comes to choosing a lettuce to grow it's down to personal preference, how much space you've got and how quickly you want something to be ready for eating. There are so many varieties, shapes, sizes, textures and colours, but all lettuces are fairly easy to grow providing you get the compost right. There are four main varieties: crisphead, butterhead, Cos (or Romaine) and loose-leaf, the latter being the easiest to grow. Lettuces don't need a special bed, you can put them between slower-growing vegetables and the lettuces will be picked long before other crops need more space in a container. Lettuce can be grown from seed or you can buy seedlings from a nursery or garden centre.

Quick potted guide

CONTAINER Suitable for containers, window boxes and grow bags with a minimum depth of 10 cm (4 in).

PLANT From seed in early spring or buy seedlings for planting out in early summer.

POSITION Open, warm, sheltered site with no risk of frost; avoid strong sunlight.

SOIL Fertile, non-acid, moist compost.

HARVEST Early summer onwards.

Planting and siting

- All varieties can be planted directly outside. Choose a sunny site at the required time, and fill your container with non-acid fertile compost – lime if necessary. Just before sowing, mix in some general-purpose fertilizer.
- Make a drill about 1 cm (½ in) deep and sow the seeds thinly.
- As they grow, you'll need to thin out the seedlings when the first true leaves appear and prevent slug damage. Water the day before and thin to stations about 15 to 30 cm (6 to 12 in) apart, depending on the variety. Discard the thinnings. Scatter with slug pellets or use other deterrent. In large containers, keep about 20 cm (8 in) between rows.
- Ready-raised seedlings are ideal for grow bags and other containers. Plant as above, and water well. ▶ 1

Maintenance

- Keep lettuces weed-free, well watered and do not let the compost dry out.
- Birds may be a problem, so erect some netting or other protection.
- In a very hot summer, you may have to provide some shelter from full sun as the leaves will wilt quickly in the heat. ▶ 2
- As winter approaches, protect over-wintering varieties with cloches; these do not have to be so well watered.

Possible problems

Slugs, snails and greenfly are the most likely pests (see pages 18–9).

Harvesting, storing and freezing

Lettuces are traditionally harvested in the morning when they have a dew on them and the leaves have not been weakened by the sun. Those with a firm head are usually ready when they feel full and solid. If they are left in the ground too long, they will run to seed. Pull or cut crispheads, butterheads and Cos at the base of the stem, as required. For loose-leaf, either cut whole or pick a few leaves as required (the thin stalks will re-shoot). Whole lettuces can be kept in the fridge for two to five days (firmer heads keep the longest) but ideally are best used as soon as possible after picking. Lettuce is not suitable for freezing.

▶ PRODUCE USED ON PAGES 111 & 125

Other salad leaves

Corn salad (Lamb's lettuce or Mache) (*Valerianella locusta, V. eriocarpa*)

Land cress (American cress or Winter cress) (*Barbarea verna*)

Rocket (Arugula and Rucola) (*Eruca sativa, E. versicaria*)

If you want to liven up your salad bowl with different flavours and textures, the most cost-effective way is to grow your own favourite varieties of individual salad leaves. The leaves require a cooler climate and don't like too much heat. You'll find several types to choose from and they all grow in a similar way. You can buy seeds or ready-grown seedlings of some varieties.

CORN SALAD (LAMB'S LETTUCE OR MACHE) A gourmet salad leaf with tender soft green leaves and a delicate fresh lettucy flavour. It grows easily and if covered it will survive throughout the winter months so gives excellent value. French varieties look like tiny compact lettuces and can be lifted whole and used as a garnish or added to a salad; other varieties are more vigorous and spreading.

LAND CRESS (AMERICAN CRESS OR WINTER CRESS) If you like watercress, then this leaf looks and tastes like watercress and is excellent for peppering-up a winter salad, or it can be cooked into a sauce or soup. It thrives in damp, shaded areas and is frost-hardy.

ROCKET (ARUGULA AND RUCOLA) This has now become one of our staple salad leaves. It can be relatively expensive to buy, so this is definitely one of the best-value leaves to grow yourself. Often classed as a herb, it can also be lightly cooked like spinach, and its small, dark green, slightly feathery leaves have a spicy, peppery flavour. Easy to grow, although the leaves seed quickly and need frequent watering.

Planting and siting

- All these seeds are best sown directly into an outdoor container. They can be grown as a 'filling-in' crop in between other vegetables, which in turn will act as a natural shield from any harsh sunlight.
- To grow on their own, divide a full container of fertile, non-acid compost, with a trickle of sand or a line of pebbles. Sow different seeds liberally and evenly in each division but don't sow too thickly. Cover with a light layer of compost. ◀ 1
- If you want different leaves to mature at the same time, make sure you check the germination times. For example, corn salad takes longer to mature than rocket, so sow these seeds a few days before rocket in order to be ready at the same time.
- As they grow, you only need to thin out the seedlings if you want larger leaves; simply cut when required.

Maintenance

- Keep the container weed-free and the leaves should be well watered. Do not allow the compost to dry out.

- Shelter from the sun if necessary. Try protecting with fleece to shield from strong sunlight as this causes the leaves to wilt (see step 2 on page 71).
- Birds may be a problem, so erect some netting or other protection.
- As winter approaches, protect over-wintering varieties with cloches; these do not have to be so well watered.

Possible problems

Usually trouble-free apart from birds, but rocket can attract flea beetle (see pages 18–9).

Harvesting, storing and freezing

All salad leaves are best picked and used as required. None of them keeps well, although you can submerge the leaves in a bowl of cold water in the fridge and keep for up to 24 hours if necessary. Either pick off individual leaves so that the plants will shoot up again, or remove the whole plants. For land cress, pick the outer leaves first, leaving the centre to produce more. As salad leaves get older, the leaves toughen, so only use the centre leaves. Salad leaves are not suitable for freezing. ◀ 2

▶ PRODUCE USED ON PAGE 114

Quick potted guide

CONTAINER Suitable for all containers and window boxes with a minimum depth of 10 cm (4 in).

PLANT From seed in spring, later summer to early autumn (depending on variety).

POSITION Cool site, not too hot; avoid strong sunlight.

SOIL Fertile, non-acid, moist compost.

HARVEST Late summer, autumn, winter (depending on variety).

Cucumber and Gherkin

(Cucumis sativus)

Quick potted guide

CONTAINER Suitable for large containers with a minimum depth of 20 cm (8 in).

PLANT From seed in late spring or buy seedlings for planting out in early summer.

POSITION Warm, sunny, sheltered site with no risk of frost.

SOIL Very rich, well-drained compost.

HARVEST Mid to late summer.

No salad is complete without the crisp, juicy cucumber. For container growing, the hardier, tougher ridged-skin cucumbers that grow outdoors are the best choice, and choose a bushy variety rather than a climber. Gherkins are small, ridged cucumbers which are ideal for pickling, as well as using as a salad vegetable. Apart from the usual dark green skinned varieties, you will also find yellow or white cucumbers, short and fat ones, and even round fruit. Most varieties are frost-tender and need long spells of warmth to grow properly. Cucumbers and gherkins can be raised from seed or from ready-grown seedlings.

Planting and siting

- All cucumber seeds need to be germinated indoors. Sow as thinly as possible in individual modules or pots as described on page 14. In order to germinate, the temperature needs to be between 20–25°C (68–77°F). Cover with a propagator lid for best results.
- As the seedlings develop, place them in cooler conditions, still light, but not in bright sunlight.
- Gradually accustom the plants to outdoor temperatures for two to three weeks before planting in the container.
- When there is no risk of frost, plant seedlings into your chosen containers – one per pot is recommended. Scatter slug pellets around or a similar deterrent.
- When the first six or seven leaves have formed, pinch out the top to encourage the plant to bush out. Take care not to damage or remove any of the male flowers (the ones bearing no fruit) as these are needed for pollination. ▶ 1 & 2

Maintenance

- Keep weeded and water generously around the seedlings, not on them.
- Renew slugs pellets or similar regularly.
- Once the fruits swell, feed with a high-potash feed every two weeks.

Possible problems

Slugs and snails can be devastating if they chew through the stems. Cucumber mosaic virus may be a possibility (see page 19).

Harvesting, storing and freezing

If left alone, cucumbers will grow to huge proportions but the flavour will deteriorate, therefore, they are best cut when they reach the recommended size – this will depend on the variety – but is usually from the end of July to the middle of September. Pick gherkins when they are about 5 to 8 cm (2 to 3 in) long. If you pick cucumbers and gherkins frequently, you will encourage more fruit to form. Cut the fruit from the stem using a sharp knife and avoid tugging as you may damage the plant. As with all watery vegetables, they are best cut and used immediately. Large cucumbers will keep for two to three days tightly wrapped in plastic wrap in the fridge, but gherkins start to soften quite quickly, so are best preserved or eaten the day they are picked. Neither variety is suitable for freezing.

▶ PRODUCE USED ON PAGES 106 & 107

Sprouting seeds

Packed full of vitamins and minerals, the little sprouts are simply the 'just-germinated' seeds of specific varieties of plant. In fact, sprouting seeds are probably one of the first things any of us have ever tried growing – how many of you sowed cress (Polycress) seeds on wads of blotting paper at school? Growing them yourself is cost-effective and the most healthy way to eat them as you simply have to snip them, give them a quick rinse and then enjoy their fresh taste. They can be ready to eat in as little as five days from sowing. A jam jar is all you need, but you will find specialist seed sprouters if you prefer. Try sprouting alfalfa, aduki bean, broccoli, chickpea, cress, fenugreek, green lentil, mung bean or mustard seeds. All add their own taste and texture to any salad or sandwich. Eat raw for maximum nutritional benefit, but they can withstand a very quick stir-fry if added towards the end of cooking.

Quick potted guide

CONTAINER Jam jar, growing mat, tray, shallow dish or specialist 'propagator'.

PLANT From seed all year round.

POSITION Warmth and light, but not full sun.

SOIL None, just water.

HARVEST All year round.

Planting and siting

- Put 1 tablespoon of your chosen variety of sprouting seeds or pulses into a large, broad-based, clean jam jar. Cover with cold water, and leave overnight on a warm windowsill, covered with a clean tea towel or some kitchen paper.
- The next day, strain the seeds through a sieve and rinse in cold water. Rinse out the jar and return the seeds to the jar. Cover the top of the jar with a piece of muslin and secure with an elastic band. Pour cold water through the muslin on to the seeds. Leave overnight. ▶ **1**
- The next day, without removing the muslin, pour the soaking water out, leave the jar for a further two to four days until the seeds have sprouted, repeating the rinsing at least twice a day.
- For purpose-built seed propagators, follow the manufacturer's instructions for best results.
- Alfalfa, cress and mustard seeds can be grown on damp kitchen paper in a small tray or shallow dish. Simply line your dish with a thin wad of kitchen paper, wet it thoroughly and drain off the excess water. Scatter the seeds evenly and not too thickly, all over the paper. Put in a warm, light place for about a week to develop. Keep the paper moist but not soaking. ▶ **2**

Maintenance

- Keep the seeds moist but not too wet.
- Keep out of direct sunlight and away from excessive heat.
- Remove any moulding sprouts; if the seeds develop a sour smell, discard the whole batch and start again with fresh seeds.

Possible problems

Sprouting seeds are trouble-free.

Harvesting, storing and freezing

Sprouting seeds take between five and 10 days to grow in ideal conditions. Harvest the shoots when they are about 2.5 cm (1 in) high, just as the green leaves begin to appear. Simply snip off sprouts from the paper base using a pair of scissors. Rinse all sprouts well before eating, and pat dry with kitchen paper. Best eaten as soon after harvesting as possible for maximum health benefits, although the sprouts can be kept in a sealed bag in the fridge for two to three days. Sprouting seeds are not suitable for freezing.

▶ PRODUCE USED ON PAGES 111 & 117

Tomato

(*Lycopersicon esculentum*)

Like the home-grown carrot, a tomato fresh off the vine has a marked difference in flavour compared to anything you can buy. The fresh smell and the juicy sweetness of the home-grown fruit can't be matched. Whilst some varieties of tomato will only grow in the heat of a greenhouse, there are plenty that will grow outdoors, and these are most suitable for container growing. Vine tomatoes grow off a sturdy main stem and need supporting on a frame or cane. Bush varieties don't need support; they are sprawling in habit which makes them ideal for pots and planters. Mini and micro-mini fruited varieties are perfect for tumbling out of hanging baskets and window boxes. You can raise tomatoes from seed but more usually, small plants are purchased from a nursery or garden centre.

Planting and siting

- When choosing your potted seedlings, select dark and perky-looking green foliage with a well-formed stem. Keep the seedlings well watered and warm indoors until they are mature enough to plant out. ◀ 1
- Even outdoor tomatoes are a tender crop, so choose the warmest, sunniest position for growing them. Usually, June is the right time for planting out, but if the weather is still on the cool side, wait a couple of weeks longer.
- Water the compost just before planting and mix in some general-purpose fertilizer.
- For tumbling and bush varieties that will be planted in hanging baskets, make holes in the compost slightly larger than the size of the pot in which the seedlings were raised. Ensure that the top of the compost ball (the compost that clings to the roots of the plant when you take it out of its container) is set just below the compost surface. Put between one and three tumblers per hanging basket, depending on variety and size of the basket. Plant bush tomatoes, one per pot or at a distance of about 20 cm (8 in) apart in larger containers or window boxes. Tumblers and bush tomatoes need no support and you do not need to remove any shoots as they grow. Water well after planting. ◀ 2
- For vine (or cordon) varieties, you will need to put in an appropriate height support for each plant in your chosen container, and tie the stem loosely to the cane. Water well after planting. Continue to tie in the stem as it grows and remove any side shoots that appear. Once the plant reaches the top of the cane, pinch out the top.

Maintenance

- Keep tomato containers weed-free and well watered.
- Feed with a high-potash fertilizer every 10 days once the fruit begins to swell.

Possible problems

Outdoor tomatoes can suffer from potato blight and mosaic virus
(see pages 18–9).

Harvesting, storing and freezing

Outdoor tomatoes are ready for picking from August through to October.
If tomatoes are left on the plants to ripen, the flavour is slightly better,
but they will carry on ripening after picking. Hold the tomato in your
hand and press the stalk with your fingers to break it neatly at the joint
just above the fruit. Some recipes call for tomatoes still on the vine, so
in these circumstances, snip off a few tomatoes still attached to the stalk.
Tomatoes will keep for a few days once ripe in the fridge, but are best
enjoyed as fresh as possible. If they have been chilled, allow them to
come back to room temperature before eating.

    If frost threatens, pick all tomatoes and put them on a sunny windowsill
to ripen them indoors. You can also put them in a paper bag with a ripe
banana to hasten ripening. Tomatoes are best frozen cooked as a sauce,
purée or as part of a recipe.

▶ PRODUCE USED ON PAGES 112, 114 & 120

Quick potted guide

CONTAINER Suitable for all
containers and window boxes
with a minimum depth of 10 cm
(4 in) for mini varieties, or 20 cm
(8 in) for bush and standard
types.

PLANT Mid spring.

POSITION Very sunny (preferably
south facing), sheltered site.

SOIL Light, slightly acid, well-
drained, fertile compost.

HARVEST Late summer onwards.

Apple

(Malus domestica)

Quick potted guide

CONTAINER Suitable for large containers with a minimum depth of 40 cm (15 in).

PLANT Ideally in October to March, but anytime as long as the conditions are favourable.

POSITION Open, sunny position, but will need protection in harsh conditions.

SOIL Rich, fertile, heavy compost.

PRUNING In winter; once established, may require additional summer pruning to maintain shape.

HARVEST August to October, depending on variety.

Small or dwarf varieties of fruit trees have been developed specifically for container growing; they have a small rootstock which means they won't grow into a large tree. Apple trees are usually raised from saplings available from nurseries and garden centres which will usually take two to three years to bear fruit. It can be a bit daunting choosing a variety to grow, but go to a specialist nursery and ask their advice. Whilst more self-pollinating trees are being developed each year, most apple trees need another variety to pollinate them. You may need two compatible varieties in order to get fruit, so check before you purchase.

Planting and siting

- When choosing your site, remember that the container will be very heavy when full so it will likely be in the same position for several years. An open, sunny site is preferable. Mix plenty of organic matter into the compost.
- Plant young trees with bare roots at any time between autumn and early spring, when the weather is favourable, but trees specially raised for containers may be planted at any time, unless the conditions are extreme.
- Make a hole one-third wider than the tree's root system in the container and firmly push in a stake, just off centre, for support.
- For bare roots, spread them carefully. You may find it easier to rest the tree on your shoulder as you start filling with compost, firming as you go, to make sure the tree is stable. Continue filling with compost until you have reached the compost mark on the tree trunk (see step 1 on page 87).
- For container-grown specimens, soak the root ball for 1 hour before planting, prepare a hole the same size as the root ball (adding a stake if required). Tease out any matted roots and plant so that the top of the root ball is level with the compost surface. Replace compost around the root ball, firm in and water well.
- Apply a rubber tree tie to the stake and wind round the trunk to secure (see step 1 on page 82).

Maintenance

- Make sure any newly planted tree doesn't dry out; keep well watered.
- Good drainage is important, so raise the pot on bricks if necessary.
- Mulch around the bottom of the trunk each spring with organic matter.
- If a late frost threatens, protect blossoms with fleece, but it is better to choose a late-flowering variety if the weather is extreme. ▶ 1
- Once the apples form, in spring or summer, thin them out if the tree is over-cropping so that none of the apples are touching. ▶ 2
- 'Top dress' the top layer of the container compost once a year to help prolong the life of the tree. In late winter/early spring, scrape away

as much of the old compost as possible without disturbing or exposing the roots. Replace with fresh compost mixed with a slow-release (high-potash) plant food. Avoid high nitrogen fertilizers as these encourage foliage rather than flowers and fruit (see step 2 on page 82).

■ To prune, always follow the aftercare and maintenance advice that is supplied with your tree, but as a general rule, in the first winter after planting, keep all sound wood but cut out all weak wood. Cut back the main top shoot and the other upper shoots to 18 cm (7 in) from where they join the central trunk and always cut just above a bud. Cut lower shoots to within 24 cm (10 in) of the joints. For a more established tree, cut back all new branches to 18 cm (7 in) from where they join the previous year's wood, and also prune in summer to maintain a good shape. ▶ 3

Possible problems

Apple trees can be susceptible to several pests and ailments but the most common are wasps, birds, canker and codling moths (see pages 18–9).

Harvesting, storing and freezing

To tell whether an apple is ready to pick, put the palm of your hand underneath it and then lift and gently twist the apple at the same time: it should easily come away with stalk attached. Apples for immediate use are best stored in the fridge for up to two weeks. Picked apples will deteriorate in warm conditions. Only late-season apples will store over winter months and they must be in perfect condition. Wrap individually in newspaper and lay in a single layer, paper folds downwards, on aerated shelves or a ventilated box. Keep in a cool, dark place and check regularly.

For freezing, peel, core and slice. Place in a bowl with 1 tablespoon of salt to every 1.2 L (2 pt) cold water to prevent discolouration. Rinse before blanching in boiling water for 30 seconds, drain well and cool. Open-freeze on lined trays until frozen and then pack into freezer bags or containers. Keep for up to 12 months. Can be used straight from the freezer in pies, compotes, etc. Stewed or puréed apple should be cooled and then packed into freezer containers. It will keep for up to 12 months. Defrost in the refrigerator overnight before using.

▶ PRODUCE USED ON PAGES 131 & 137

Cherry

(Prunus species)

Cherry trees are traditionally big trees and for this reason cherries are not as popular as apples to grow. However, there are now several varieties of smaller trees available which can be pot grown; they are easy to protect from birds and take up less space. You'll find sweet cherry varieties for eating (it is best to choose a self-fertile variety because it is more complicated trying to pollinate a cherry tree than other orchard fruit), and sour varieties for cooking and preserving; the latter are self-fertile so you'll only need one tree, they are more hardy and are most often the smallest of cherry trees. Cherry trees are usually raised from saplings or ready-mature small trees available from nurseries and garden centres. If you are unsure about the suitability of the variety, ask the nursery before purchasing.

Planting and siting

- When choosing your site, remember that the container will be very heavy when full so it will likely be in the same position for several years. All cherry trees like the sun and warmth, so a south facing spot is ideal, but sour cherry trees can tolerate cooler climates and less sun. No cherry tree likes very wet or cold conditions.
- The compost in your container needs to be well drained but able to retain some moisture – not waterlogged though.
- The preparation and planting instructions are the same for cherries as with apples (see pages 80–1).

Maintenance

- Mulch with organic matter to help improve moisture levels in the compost and give nutrients to the tree.
- Make sure your newly planted tree doesn't dry out and keep well watered, weed-free and well-supported. ◀ 1
- Cherry trees do not require thinning. As the fruits begin to colour, protect the tree from birds by draping netting over the tree (see step 1 on pages 80–1).
- 'Top dress' or replace the top layer of the container compost once a year in order to prolong the life of the tree.◀ 2
- Sweet cherry trees require little pruning apart from removing dead or damaged wood or crossing branches. The fruit forms on spurs on two-year-old and more mature wood. Mature trees require a summer pruning to restrict foliage and encourage fruit buds to form.
- Sour cherries grow on new wood, so once the fruit is harvested, cut back the branches where the fruit has been to half their length. Remove dead or damaged wood or crossing branches. In early summer, reduce the number of new shoots to about one every 7 cm (3 in).
- Remove any shoots from the main trunk or the bottom of the tree by pulling rather than cutting.

Possible problems

Birds are the biggest pest, whilst aphids may also attack. Silver leaf and brown rot are the most common diseases (see pages 18–9)

Harvesting, storing and freezing

Sweet cherries can be easily pulled off the stalks by hand. Choose a cool time of the day so that the leaves are not wilting and dropping over and hiding the fruit. Sour cherries should be cut off with stalk intact to prevent being damaged. Both types should either be eaten or used in cooking on the same day as picking for best results, but will keep unwashed for a two to three days in the fridge if necessary.

Fresh cherries can be frozen like raspberries, but they do lose some texture once thawed. Cooked cherries can also be frozen successfully.

▶ PRODUCE USED ON PAGE 127

Quick potted guide

CONTAINER Suitable for large containers with a minimum depth of 45 cm (18 in).

PLANT Ideally in October to March but anytime as long as the conditions are favourable.

POSITION Sunny, sheltered position.

SOIL Well drained, light, fertile compost but able to retain some moisture.

PRUNING Sour cherries (spring and summer); sweet cherries (summer).

HARVEST July to September, depending on variety.

Pear

(Pyrus communis)

Pears need more sun and water than apples. Pear trees flower earlier and are best kept in a sheltered position in case of a late frost – choose a late-flowering variety if frost is a risk. They like to be pruned more than an apple tree and you'll find varieties available for container growing (choose ones with a Pixie rootstock). Pears are not usually self-fertile; however, new developments are made all the time and with a bit of effort you should be able to find at least one variety that is. Otherwise you will need two compatible plants that flower at the same time in order to make them fruit. Different varieties fruit from August through to the end of October. Pear trees are usually raised from saplings or ready-mature small trees available from nurseries and garden centres. Seek specialist advice before purchase if you are unsure about the suitability of the variety.

Planting and siting

- Choose a sheltered, sunny site, and the compost should have good drainage but be able to retain some moisture.

Quick potted guide

CONTAINER Suitable for large containers with a minimum depth of 45 cm (18 in).

PLANT Ideally in October to March but anytime as long as the conditions are favourable.

POSITION Sunny, sheltered position.

SOIL Well-drained, fertile compost able to retain some moisture.

PRUNING In July, and in November to February.

HARVEST August to October, depending on variety.

■ The preparation and planting instructions are the same for pears as with apples (see pages 80–1).

Maintenance

■ Pears require the same protection, watering, feeding, mulching and thinning as apples (see steps 1 and 2 on pages 80–1).

■ 'Top dress' or replace the top layer of the container compost once a year in order to prolong the life of the tree (see step 2 on page 82).

■ To prune, young pear trees follow a three-year cycle. In the first year, side shoots called laterals grow around the main stems of the tree; in the second year, fruit buds will form on these shoots; and in the third year, they will fruit. Once fruit has formed and been harvested, cut the lateral shoots back to within 2.5 cm (1 in) of the main stem; this will encourage new, stronger lateral shoots to form and fruit in another three years, which will, in turn, require the same pruning regime. As the main stems continue to grow, they will produce more laterals, and fruiting will be continuous each year.

■ In winter, cut out intertwined branches and spurs, and remove weak, dead or damaged growth. Always follow the aftercare advice and maintenance routine that is supplied with your tree.

Possible problems

Pear trees are susceptible to the same pests and diseases as apples, along with canker and brown rot (see pages 18–9).

Harvesting, storing and freezing

Most pears ripen off the tree. Early varieties need cutting from the tree when the fruit is mature but still hard. Mid- and late-season fruits can be picked by gently twisting from the tree. ▶ 1

Pears for storing don't need wrapping. Arrange in a single layer, not touching, on a shelf or tray lined with a cardboard-moulded fruit tray to keep them spaced apart. They should be in perfect condition and need frequent checking. Once the fruit begins to soften at the stalk end, bring indoors and store at about 16°C (61°F) for two to three days to complete the ripening. ▶ 2

If frozen, pears discolour and become watery after thawing. Freeze as a purée or poach in a heavy sugar syrup and added lemon juice for best results.

▶ PRODUCE USED ON PAGE 131

Plum

(Prunus domestica)

Quick potted guide

CONTAINER Suitable for large containers with a minimum depth of 45 cm (18 in).

PLANT Ideally in November to March but anytime as long as the conditions are favourable.

POSITION Sheltered, sunny position.

SOIL Rich, fertile, moisture-retentive compost but can tolerate drier conditions than other orchard fruits.

PRUNING Summer.

HARVEST August to September.

A juicy, rich-flavoured fruit, plums grow in much the same way as pears, but unlike pears, there are several self-fertilizing varieties available. In general, plum trees like sun, warmth, shelter and good drainage; they flower early so choose a variety suitable for a more extreme climate if you have late frosts. Plums are mainly grown as trees or bushes, and there are several varieties suitable for container growing which have a dwarfing rootstock. Plums are usually raised from saplings or ready-mature small trees available from nurseries and garden centres. As with all fruit trees, seek specialist advice before purchase if you are unsure about the variety.

Planting and siting

■ Choose an open sunny site in an area where there is no chance of a late frost. In a cooler climate, it would be better to choose a site next to a sunny wall for more protection. Make sure the compost is fertile and moisture-retentive by digging in plenty of organic material.

■ The preparation and planting instructions are the same as for apples and pears (see pages 80–1). ▶ 1

Maintenance

■ Plums require the same protecting, watering, feeding and mulching as for apples and pears (see step 1 on pages 80–1).

■ If the fruit yield is heavy, start thinning the fruit as soon as the stones form and thin to about 5 cm (2 in) apart (see step 2 on pages 80–1).

■ For pruning, these trees are pruned in July and August to lower the risk of infection by silver leaf (see page 19), especially in cooler climates. A golden rule is: only prune when really necessary. Plum trees produce fruit at the base of one-year-old shoots, as well as on wood and spurs that are two years old. Once you have the right shape, simply prune any retained new growth to six leaves from where the new stalk emerges from the old wood, and remove crossing or overcrowded branches along with any diseased or damaged wood by taking it back to healthy wood. ▶ 2

Possible problems

Wasps and birds can be a problem as well as aphids. More problematical diseases are silver leaf, canker and brown rot (see pages 18–9).

Harvesting, storing and freezing

Harvest time for plums is August to September. Pick plums for cooking, preserving and freezing before they are quite ripe. For eating, leave them on the tree to ripen fully and they will be sweeter for it. If the weather is excessively wet, it is advisable to pick the fruit to avoid the skins splitting. Pull the fruit away from the tree with the stalk intact. As with all fruit, plums are best used as soon after picking as possible. ▶ 3

Fresh plums aren't suitable for freezing as the skin will be tough once thawed. They are best cut in half, then poached and stored in rigid containers topped with a heavy sugar syrup and added lemon juice, or in cooked or puréed form.

▶ PRODUCE USED ON PAGE 117

Blueberry

(Vaccinium corymbosum)

The native bilberry or blaeberry has grown wild for years in parts of the northern hemisphere, but over the last decade or so, the American 'high bush' blueberry has become popular. This cultivated variety produces bigger fruit in greater quantities and is an attractive addition to any garden. The blueberry plant needs lots of moist, acid compost to grow, and for this reason, it is often suggested that the plants are grown in pots rather than the ground. Blueberry bushes take a while to crop well, but after about five years, an established bush produces a fair yield. The foliage turns a beautiful red in autumn for a much-needed splash of colour. The plants are frost-hardy, but you will need to protect the fruit from the birds. Blueberries are raised from small plants available from nurseries and garden centres.

Quick potted guide

CONTAINER Suitable for medium and large containers with a minimum depth of 45 cm (18 in).

PLANT In winter (November to March).

POSITION Sunny spot to ripen fruit, but can tolerate slight shade.

SOIL Acid, rich, free-draining, fertile compost.

PRUNING November to March.

HARVEST Midsummer/early autumn, depending on variety.

Planting and siting

- Choose a sunny site, although light shade can be tolerated. The compost must be acidic (between pH 4 and 5.5) so it is best to use ericaceous compost in your container. Fertilize with sulphate of potash or sulphate of ammonia, and avoid anything containing lime or calcium.
- Plant from late autumn to late winter when conditions are favourable.
- Soak the potted specimen plant in a bucket of rainwater for 1 hour before planting.
- Make a hole in your chosen container slightly larger than the pot of your specimen and ease the plant out of its pot into the hole. Plant one bush per container. Cover the roots with about 5 cm (2 in) compost and firm down gently. ▶ 1

Maintenance

- As the plant matures, mulch with moist ericaceous compost or leaf mould to help retain moisture. Do not allow the compost to become dry. ▶ 2
- Water with rainwater to maintain acid levels.
- Protect with netting to keep birds away from the fruit.
- Blueberries grow on the second or third year wood stems, so do not prune until the first crop is complete. Then, in the following winter or early spring, cut out any dead or weak wood, and take out up to one-third of the oldest stems to help promote new growth.

Possible problems

Apart from birds, chlorosis can be a problem (see page 18).

Harvesting, storing and freezing

Berries should be ready to pick from mid-July to September. Harvest over a few weeks when they are evenly blue and have a slight bloom. ▶ 3 They will not ripen after harvest, so avoid any with a green tinge or reddish colour near the stem as this indicates that they are unripe. You'll need to go over each plant several times in order to make sure you harvest all the berries. As with all berries, eat them as soon after picking as you can. Otherwise, store unwashed in the fridge for 24 hours, if required, and wash just before using. Blueberries freeze like raspberries and can be cooked straight from frozen (see page 97), they do soften on defrosting if using uncooked.

▶ PRODUCE USED ON PAGES 127 & 138

Cranberry

(Vaccinium oxycoccos)

Tangy berries, rich in vitamin C and a staple of the Thanksgiving and Christmas dinner table. The plants are low-growing, creeping evergreen shrubs that grow best in damp, acidic compost and are ideal for containers as long as they are kept moist and damp. Cranberries can be grown as trailing plants in hanging baskets, and the delicate late spring flowers and colourful autumn foliage make the cranberry an attractive all year round plant. When buying cranberry plants, make sure you buy mature plants: most varieties won't produce a good crop of berries until they are at least two years old. Mature plants are available from specialist nurseries.

Quick potted guide

CONTAINER Suitable for all containers with a minimum depth of 20 cm (8 in).

PLANT In spring.

POSITION Sun or partial shade; avoiding strong sunlight which will quickly dry the plant out.

SOIL Acid, rich, moisture-retentive, fertile compost.

HARVEST From September until the first frost.

Planting and siting

- In spring, choose a sunny or partially shaded site. The compost must be acidic (between pH 4 and 5.5) so it is best to use ericaceous compost in your container. Fertilize with sulphate of potash or sulphate of ammonia, and avoid anything containing lime or calcium. Make sure the compost is moist before planting.
- Soak your plant in a container of rainwater for about 1 hour before planting. ▶ 1
- Make a hole in the compost in your container the same size as the plant pot and plant one bush per container. Firm down gently. Don't expect too much from the bush in the first couple of years. ▶ 2
- Planting several bushes at once if space permits will help encourage pollination.

Maintenance

- Protect with netting to keep birds away from the fruit, especially when the weather gets colder.
- Cranberries need plenty of water; they should be kept moist with rainwater but take care not to 'drown' your plant.
- Add a pinch of food every month during the growing period in the spring and summer.
- Very little pruning is necessary: simply trim back straggling stalks into shape after the fruit has been harvested.
- The container lifespan of a cranberry bush is about three years, and plants may need replacing or repotting with more ericaceous compost after this time.

Possible problems

Apart from birds, chlorosis can be a problem (see page 18).

Harvesting, storing and freezing

Fruits will ripen from September, and are best picked before the first frost, when the colour is even all over. ▶ 3 Cranberries will keep for weeks if picked on the vine and it's possible to keep them this way in the fridge for Christmas – wash just before using. Cranberries are not eaten raw and require plenty of sugar to sweeten them when cooked. Cranberries freeze like raspberries and are best cooked straight from frozen (see page 97).

▶ PRODUCE USED ON PAGE 131

Currants

black-, red- and white

(Ribes nigrum and Ribes sativum)

The blackcurrant is the hardiest of the currant family and does well in any part of the country. It is easy to grow and lives for up to 10 years. Blackcurrants like to be free-standing and are quite bushy, so look for compact bush varieties for your container. Red- and white currants can be trained, making them an ideal choice if you are short on space, and they are just as easy to grow as blackcurrants. All currants are raised from bushes available from nurseries and garden centres.

Planting and siting

- Choose a sunny sheltered site for your container and fill with rich, moisture-retentive compost with plenty of well-rotted organic material added to it.
- Plant the bushes between autumn and early spring when the weather is favourable. Soak the plant in a container of water for 1 hour before planting.
- Make a hole wide enough to spread out the roots and deep enough so that the old compost mark is 5 cm (2 in) below the surface. Plant one bush per container.
- After planting blackcurrants, cut down all shoots to one bud to encourage new growth. For red- and white currants, if there are any side shoots after planting, cut them back to one bud, otherwise do not cut back after planting. ◀ 1

Maintenance

- Red- and white currants produce suckers as they grow – these should be pulled off (not cut off) the stem or root in June or July whilst the wood is soft.
- Mulch all currants in spring with well-rotted organic matter, as well as potassium (and nitrogen for blackcurrants) fertilizers.
- Water in dry weather but not as the fruit ripens as this may cause it to split.
- Protect currants with netting or other bird protection once the fruit forms.
- Regular pruning is essential to maintain high yields. Red- and white currants are best grown in open-centre bushes in pots (for pruning, see Gooseberry on page 95).
- The first winter after planting blackcurrants, cut out or cut back any weak wood. Continue removing dead or weak wood each winter along with up to one-third of the older wood – this will encourage new growth – and avoid keeping any branches for more than four years. As a guide, new shoots are beige in colour, whilst older wood is grey/black in colour. If you reduce the length of new shoots you will inhibit fruit formation. ◀ 2

Possible problems

Apart from birds, aphids and botrytis may be a problem (see pages 18–9).

Harvesting, storing and freezing

Pick blackcurrants when they are fully ripe – this will be about a week after they turn glossy black. The ones at the top of the stems will be the ripest. Red- and white currants need picking as soon as they ripen; they spoil quickly and do not keep for long, and become difficult to pick cleanly if too ripe. Currants should be used as soon after picking as possible. Wash just before using.

All currants can be frozen, stripped from the stalks, washed, dried and packed into rigid containers. They will keep for up to 12 months and can be used from frozen for pies, puddings and jam. They freeze well in small clusters: best open-frozen and then packed into containers – these defrost well for using as garnishes. Alternatively, freeze with sugar by layering dry in rigid containers with 115 g (4 oz) sugar per 450 g (1 lb) red- or white currants, or 150–175 g (5½–6 oz) for blackcurrants, for use in pies and desserts. Currants can also be stewed with sugar in a little water, then cooled and frozen as they are, or strained to make purée.

▶ PRODUCE USED ON PAGES 127 & 128

Quick potted guide

CONTAINER Suitable for medium and large containers with a minimum depth of 30 cm (12 in).

PLANT In winter (November to March).

POSITION Sunny spot to ripen fruit; blackcurrants will tolerate light shade. Shelter from cold and drying wind.

SOIL Rich, moisture-retentive, fertile compost.

PRUNING Winter and summer, depending on variety.

HARVEST June to August.

Gooseberry

(Ribes uva-crispa)

A native plant to northern Europe in general. It is very hardy and provides us with one of the first berry fruits of the season. Gooseberries are easy to grow in bush form or can be trained more formally into cordons or standards. There are several varieties to choose from, some with sweet or sour berries, large or small in size and white, yellow, green and red in colour. Standards are the best choice for containers. Gooseberries are raised from small bushes available from nurseries and garden centres.

Planting and siting

- Choose an open sunny site for your container, although gooseberries will tolerate light shade. The compost should be richly fertilized with well-rotted manure.
- Plant the bushes between autumn and early spring when the weather is favourable. Soak the plant in a container of water for 1 hour before planting.
- Make a hole in the compost in your container just large enough to avoid disturbing the roots of your plant, but not too deep. Carefully cover the roots with compost and firm in gently. Plant one bush per container. ▶ 1
- If there are any side shoots after planting, cut them back to one bud.

Maintenance

- Gooseberries produce suckers as they grow – these should be pulled off (not cut off) the stem or root in June or July whilst the wood is soft.

Quick potted guide

CONTAINER Suitable for medium and large containers with a minimum depth of 30 cm (12 in).

PLANT October to March.

POSITION Open, sunny or partially shaded spot but shelter if very hot.

SOIL Fertile, well-drained, moist compost.

PRUNING Winter and summer.

HARVEST Late May to August, depending on variety.

- Take care when weeding around gooseberry bushes, because they are shallow-rooted and easily damaged.
- Gooseberries require high potassium levels and regular mulching with well-rotted manure.
- New shoots are prone to bird damage and also need protecting from strong winds, so netting and windbreak protection may need to be erected.
- Water in dry weather but not as the fruit ripens as this may cause it to split.
- Heavy-cropping plants should start to be thinned out from May onwards, removing berries from each branch to encourage those left behind to swell further (use the unripe fruit for jam making).
- Gooseberry bushes require pruning to keep them in shape. Wear gloves as the stems are spiky. In winter, remove damaged wood or crossing branches. Cut the previous year's growth back to two buds and remove any shoots or crossing branches from the centre to keep an open structure. Each year, follow the same procedure but increase the number of branches in the main frame. Cut back new growth on the main stems by about half in winter, and reduce the side shoots on the remaining stems down to two buds. Any central or other unwanted shoots can be cut out from June onwards if necessary. ▶ **2**

Possible problems

Apart from birds, powdery mildew can be a problem (see pages 18–9).

Harvesting, storing and freezing

Harvesting depends on the variety but is usually from June to August; carefully pick the berries when they are beginning to yield to gentle pressure.

Gooseberries can be successfully frozen in different ways: without sugar, top and tail (snip off the flower and stalk end) with scissors. Put in a colander and wash carefully by dipping in cold water several times. Drain well and dry the berries. Freeze on trays and then pack into bags or rigid containers. Keep for up to 12 months. Cook from frozen for use in pies and puddings. With sugar, prepare as for eating, layer dry in rigid containers with 115 g (4 oz) sugar per 450 g (1 lb) gooseberries. Use in pies and desserts, or stewed with sugar – cook the gooseberries in a little water with sugar to taste. Cool and freeze as is, or strain to make a purée; pack in bags or rigid containers.

▶ PRODUCE USED ON PAGES 127 & 128

Raspberry and Blackberry

(*Rubus idaeus*)

(*Rubus fruticosus*)

Raspberries and blackberries grow in sun or partial shade. Blackberries are frost-hardy, but can be quite prolific and bushy. They are easier to grow than raspberries but produce less fruit – choose thornless varieties for containers which have a less vigorous growing habit and take up less space. Blackberries usually fruit in the second year of planting, and will live for up to 20 years. Raspberries are amongst the most well loved and tasty of all the summer berries, and grow well throughout the cooler parts of the northern hemisphere. Whilst you can grow any variety in a container, raspberries take up a fair bit of space and need a supporting structure to keep them upright, so look out for compact varieties. Both raspberries and blackberries are raised from 'canes' (a small cluster of bare-rooted stems), which are available from nurseries and garden centres.

Planting and siting

- Choose an open sunny site, although partially shaded areas are also suitable.
- Permanent supports need to be erected at the time of planting, and either trellis or a frame up against a wall or a stout bamboo cane or post in the pot will be suitable. The support needs to be able to hold the growing plant and prevent it from blowing over in the wind.
- Plant dormant, bare-rooted raspberry canes in autumn or early winter for best results, so that the canes can establish quickly. Plant bare-rooted blackberry canes during winter, or early spring if the weather is severe. Soak the canes in water for 1 hour before planting. Plant one cane per container.

Quick potted guide

CONTAINER Medium to large containers with a minimum depth of 45 cm (18 in).

PLANT From November to March.

POSITION Open sunny spot but will tolerate some shade.

SOIL Rich, fertile compost. Free-draining for blackberries, moisture-retentive for raspberries.

PRUNING September to October (blackberries); autumn and winter (raspberries).

HARVEST July to October, depending on variety.

- Don't plant the roots too deeply; spread out evenly at a depth of 5–7 cm (2 3 in), cover with compost and gently firm them in. ▶ 1
- After planting, if the canes aren't ready trimmed, immediately cut them to within 25 cm (10 in) of the ground for raspberries or down to a bud about 23 cm (9 in) above ground for blackberries.
- Secure the fruit stem to a suitable support structure or trellis. ▶ 2

Maintenance

- Keep the container weed-free.
- Add mulch during spring to prevent drying out and water in dry weather.
- Protect from birds as fruit forms.
- Raspberries produce 'suckers' that appear out of the ground. Remove them by pulling rather than cutting them from the plant.
- For summer raspberries and blackberries, after fruiting, in autumn, cut out all the old fruiting stems (brown wood) and tie the new growth (green wood) to the support system. Excess stems can be removed to give a better shape. In late winter, cut off the tip of each stem to a bud about 18 cm (7 in) above the top of the support system. For late or autumn fruiting varieties of raspberry, cut all stems to the ground in late winter. ▶ 3

Possible problems

Birds, raspberry beetle and botrytis are the most common problems (see pages 18–9).

Harvesting, storing and freezing

Blackberries fruit from July to September, according to variety, until the first frost comes, when superstition has it that the Devil spits on the berries. The best fruit forms on the previous season's shoots. Pick carefully to avoid bruising. The fruit deteriorates quickly after picking, so it is best used quickly. Pick raspberries when they are evenly and richly coloured all over. When a raspberry is harvested, the white cone-like central core remains behind on the plant; with the blackberry, the white core comes away with the rest of the berry. Eat the berries as soon after picking as possible though they will keep, loosely covered, unwashed in the fridge for 24 hours if necessary.

To freeze the berries, wash and carefully pat dry after picking. Either pack straight into bags or rigid containers, or open-freeze side by side on trays for packing later. Keep frozen for up to 12 months. Use straight from frozen but they do hold up quite well once defrosted.

▶ PRODUCE USED ON PAGES 127, 136 & 138

Strawberry

(Fragaria x ananassa)

A rewarding soft fruit to grow that is easy to maintain. There are many varieties to give the grower crops of berries from the end of May right through to October. The easiest and quickest way to raise strawberries is to buy plants from a nursery or garden centre, although alpine varieties grow well from seed. You will be able to buy plants from early spring onwards at various stages of development; mid-season strawberries give a good crop in the first year and are usually the best choice for most people. Plants produce offshoots as they grow called runners; these should be removed to conserve the plant's energy and can be potted up as plants for use next year.

Quick potted guide

CONTAINER Suitable for all containers with a minimum depth of 20 cm (8 in).

PLANT From spring to midsummer; alpine varieties: from seed in autumn to plant out the following spring.

POSITION Open, sunny spot.

SOIL Slightly acidic, rich, free-draining, fertile compost.

HARVEST End of May to late summer, depending on variety.

Planting and siting

- Choose an open, sunny site for your container. The compost should be richly fertile and well drained. Before planting, dig in plenty of general-purpose fertilizer (slightly acidic with a pH 6 to 6.5).
- Using a trowel, make a hole in the compost the same size as the pot. Make holes at intervals of about 25 cm (10 in) apart in large containers and window boxes. For hanging baskets, plant three per basket. ▶ 1
- Firm the compost to level with the base of the central crown and water in well. ▶ 2
- Alpine strawberries are grown from seed, indoors in modules in autumn. Plant seedlings 15 cm (6 in) apart when large enough to handle, in mid-spring. The plants will fruit throughout the summer.

Maintenance

- Water regularly and keep the pot weed-free. If frost threatens during flowering, cover with fleece, polythene or cloches.
- Remove runners as they form as these will sap energy from the plants – keep and repot as new plants, if desired. After fruiting, cut off all the old leaves, repot and keep in a sheltered spot until the following spring. ▶ 3
- Protect with netting to keep the birds away.

Possible problems

Birds, red spider mite, squirrels, slugs and botrytis are the most common problems (see pages 18–9).

Harvesting, storing and freezing

Pick strawberries by the stalk to avoid bruising. Eat as soon as possible after picking although they will keep unwashed in a dish for two to three days in the fridge. Leave alpine strawberries to ripen fully to develop flavour and eat on the same day as picking. Pick regularly to encourage more fruits to form. Place in a colander and rinse carefully in cold water, drain and pat dry just before serving. All strawberries are best eaten fresh as their flavour and texture change after defrosting. Freeze as for raspberries (see page 97), then defrost and blend before serving as a sauce or fold into mousses and creams.

▶ PRODUCE USED ON PAGES 127, 138 & 140

Rhubarb

(Rheum x cultorum)

Rhubarb is strictly a stem vegetable but is regarded as a fruit because it is served mostly for pudding. It grows best in an open site so that the leaves can spread out. The container needs to be big as the roots of an established plant run deep. It is easy to cultivate and a single plant will provide a good yield for a small family. Only rhubarb stalks are edible – the leaves are full of oxalic acid and are poisonous. Once a rhubarb plant has established – after three years – it can be forced for early cropping. 'Forced' rhubarb is thinner-stalked, softer and pinker than those stalks left to mature unforced, and is ready for picking from spring to early summer. Rhubarb is usually grown from a 'crown' available from a nursery or garden centre in spring.

Planting and siting

- Rhubarb is a sun-loving plant and doesn't like shade. It needs lots of rich, fertile compost to grow, and fertilizer should be dug down deep into fertile compost at the bottom of your container just before planting.

Quick potted guide

CONTAINER Suitable for large containers with a minimum depth of 45 cm (18 in).

PLANT Spring.

POSITION Open, sunny spot.

SOIL Rich, free-draining, fertile compost.

HARVEST Summer of the second year onwards.

- Rhubarb plants can be planted outside in spring or early summer if they are kept well watered. Soak the crown in a bucket of water for 1 hour before planting.
- Make a hole the size of the pot in a large container of rich compost and plant so that the bud of the crown is just below the surface. ▶ 1
- Firm the compost around the plant using the knuckles of your hand after filling the hole. Plant one crown per large container. ▶ 2

Maintenance

- Keep weed-free, water well in dry weather and remove any flowering shoots that appear.
- Apply a mulch of well-rotted manure around the plant in autumn and again in spring.
- Allow new plants to become established for 12 to 18 months after planting before pulling. A rhubarb plant will be productive for between five and 10 years.
- If you want to 'force' rhubarb for early, fine stems, cover the crown with a large upturned bucket or special terracotta rhubarb forcer in mid-winter. The sticks will be ready in about six weeks. Do not force the same plant for at least two years otherwise the plant will weaken.

Possible problems

A relatively trouble-free plant.

Harvesting, storing and freezing

Don't pick any stems in the first year. In the second year, pull a few stems, leaving about half on the plant, and stop around midsummer to allow the plant to recover. In the following years, pull fully grown stems as needed. To pull, place your thumb inside the stem as far down as you can, and twist to pull it away from the crown. Do not cut the stems. Rhubarb is best used straight from the garden, although you should be able to keep the stalks for one to two days in the fridge before they begin to wilt. ▶ 3

For freezing, choose tender young stalks and trim off the leafy tops and the pale pink root. Wash and dry thoroughly. Cut into 2.5 cm (1 in) lengths and dry pack in rigid containers or freezer bags. Blanching is unnecessary. Keep for up to six months. Use for stewed fruit and pies. Alternatively, pack as above but sprinkle with sugar in between each layer for using as a ready-to-cook compote once thawed. Rhubarb can also be frozen cooked in stewed and puréed forms.

▶ PRODUCE USED ON PAGE 130

Citrus fruit

Citrus spp.

Smaller varieties of orange, along with lemons, limes, kaffir limes and kumquats (*Fortunella margarita*) can be grown successfully in containers, outside in a warm, sunny, sheltered position, or indoors all year round. Growing in a container means plants can be easily moved out of doors on a hot day and then returned indoors as the air cools. They must have frost-free conditions. Citrus plants have spiny stems with glossy evergreen leaves; in spring, the flowers are deliciously fragrant. Most fruits take up to 12 months to develop and ripen, so it is quite usual for plants to flower whilst bearing fruit. Citrus plants are usually obtained from garden centres and specialist nurseries as developed potted plants.

Planting and siting

- After February, citrus plants start to put on new growth, so they will either need potting on into larger pots, or dressing with fresh compost if larger or more mature. For potting on, choose a pot the next size up from the existing container – citrus don't like too large a container.
- Cover the base of the pot with a 2.5 cm (1 in) depth of fine drainage material (see page 11) to ensure good drainage and add some specialist citrus compost. Place the root ball on top and fill in the edges with more compost, ensuring the top feeder roots are covered with a thin layer of fresh compost.
- Water well and keep in the shade for a few weeks to allow new roots to grow. Feed after six weeks of repotting.
- For dressing, scrape away as much of the old compost as possible without disturbing or exposing the roots, and replace with citrus compost.
- Ideal conditions should be at a minimum of 10°C (50°F) in winter, and keep in a cool, frost-free place; keep away from a central heating source though. In summer, move to a sunny position, avoiding direct sunlight for the first three weeks to prevent leaf scorch.

Maintenance

- Citrus plants are active all year round and require feeding to reflect this. Choose a high-nitrogen soluble plant food and feed monthly from spring to end of September to encourage a bushy growth habit and healthy leaves. For winter, use a balanced slow-release plant food that will help with fruit ripening and maintain health over the winter. Specialist citrus food is also available in a drip feeder. ◄ 1
- Keep pots weed-free to reduce the risk of attack from pests and disease. ◄ 2
- Citrus plants prefer slightly acidic conditions so water with rainwater or distilled water in hard water areas. Water regularly, but allow the surface to dry out between watering. Do not stand in water.
- Misting with rainwater will help keep plants cool in very hot weather and encourages pollination.

■ Prune the main branches of newly planted trees by one-third in the first year. After fruiting, prune only to remove dead, diseased or crossing branches or any that touch the compost.

Possible problems

Citrus plants grown indoors can become infested by red spider mite, whitefly and scale insects, or suffer from chlorosis (see pages 18–9).

Harvesting, storing and freezing

Harvest ripe fruits by cutting them at their stalk with secateurs, scissors or a sharp knife. Small fruits can be pulled from the plant with a gentle twist. Undamaged fruit will keep in the fridge for several weeks. Citrus fruit is not usually frozen, although the leaves of the kaffir lime can be frozen in small, well-sealed bags for up to six months and used frozen. Kumquats can be open frozen whole, then packed and frozen for up to six months; they are best used in cooking as their texture softens on defrosting.

▶ PRODUCE USED ON PAGES 107, 118, 128, 132, 134 & 140

Quick potted guide

CONTAINER Suitable for containers with a minimum depth of 20 cm (8 in) for dwarf plants, and 30 cm (12 in) for more established trees.

PLANT Repot or dress in late winter.

POSITION Sunny, sheltered, frost-free site; indoors away from a central heating source.

SOIL Rich, free-draining compost.

HARVEST Autumn/winter.

Recipes

I'm sure you've got plenty of your own **ideas** when it comes to cooking your own produce, but I've included a few of my **favourite recipes** you might like to try out on your friends and family. Over the following pages you'll find a selection of **soups, salads** and **main meals** along with some delicious **sweet dishes** and a few ideas for **preserving** some of your fruit and vegetables to enjoy out of season. I hope you enjoy cooking (and **eating**) your own!

Warm Thai pork salad

A deliciously fragrant and slightly spicy hot mixture of ingredients which can make a stunning starter as part of an Oriental meal, or spoon over rice or noodles for a main course. Use chicken or beef instead of pork if preferred.

SERVES 4

8 spring onions, trimmed and chopped

2 sweet peppers, deseeded and thinly sliced

½ cucumber, washed and sliced

Small bunch of fresh coriander

450 g (1 lb) lean pork, thinly sliced

2 garlic cloves, peeled and crushed

1 red chilli, deseeded and finely chopped

3 Tbsp dark soy sauce

2 tsp sesame oil

3 Tbsp crunchy peanut butter

1 Tbsp white rice or sherry vinegar

2 tsp clear honey

2 pak choi or 1 small Chinese cabbage, washed

1 Tbsp vegetable oil

1 Put the spring onions, pepper and cucumber in a heatproof serving bowl. Break up the coriander and mix into the salad bowl. Cover and chill until required.

2 Put the pork in a shallow dish and mix in the garlic, chilli and 1 tablespoon of soy sauce. Cover and chill for at least 30 minutes, or until ready to cook.

3 Put the remaining soy sauce, sesame oil, peanut butter, vinegar and honey in a small screw-top jar, seal and shake well to mix into a thick dressing. Set aside until ready to serve.

4 When you are ready to serve the salad, trim the pak choi or Chinese cabbage, and shred finely. Heat the vegetable oil in a wok or frying pan until hot and stir-fry the pork for 5 to 6 minutes, until just tender. Add the pak choi or cabbage and stir-fry for a further minute.

5 To serve, toss the cooked pork mixture into the prepared salad ingredients. Shake the dressing again and pour over the salad to serve. Best served whilst the pork is still warm.

FREEZING Not suitable.

 PRODUCE GROWN ON PAGES 22, 26, 40, 58, 63 & 74

Warm smoked salmon and noodle salad with delicate herbs

A pretty light supper dish that tastes good too. Yellow varieties of courgette look particularly attractive in this dish.

1 Put the noodles in a large heatproof bowl and pour over sufficient boiling water to cover. Put aside to soak for at least 10 minutes.

2 Meanwhile, trim the courgettes, slice in half lengthways and cut into thin slices. Cut the cucumber in half lengthways and thinly slice.

3 Heat the oil in a wok or large deep-frying pan and stir-fry the spring onions and courgette for 5 minutes. Add the cucumber and stir-fry for a further minute.

4 Drain the noodles thoroughly and add to the wok. Stir-fry for about 2 minutes to heat through. Remove from the heat and stir in the lemon juice, chopped herbs and smoked salmon. Season to taste.

5 Pile on to warmed serving plates. Garnish with chive flowers and serve immediately.

COOK'S NOTE Smoked cooked chicken would work well with these flavours as well, or you could try a combination of cooked shellfish.

FREEZING Not suitable.

SERVES 2
115 g (4 oz) thin ribbon rice noodles
2 courgettes, trimmed
1 small cucumber, washed
2 Tbsp cold-pressed rapeseed oil or other vegetable oil
6 spring onions, trimmed and chopped
2 Tbsp lemon juice
2 Tbsp each freshly chopped tarragon, chervil and chives
225 g (8 oz) smoked salmon, cut into thin strips
Salt and freshly ground black pepper
Few chive flowers, to garnish

▶ PRODUCE GROWN ON PAGES 26, 54, 63, 66, 74 & 102

Potage vert

Most combinations of green vegetables will work in this soup so it can be easily adapted to whatever you're growing.

SERVES 4
4 small leeks
2 medium courgettes, washed
225 g (8 oz) broccoli, washed
225 g (8 oz) spring cabbage, pak choi or other greens
1.2 L (2 pt) vegetable stock
1 bay leaf
225 g (8 oz) shelled peas
Small bunch of fresh basil
Salt and freshly ground black pepper
4 Tbsp double cream (optional)
4 Tbsp fresh pesto sauce (see Cook's note)

1 First prepare the vegetables. Trim the leeks and split them lengthways. Rinse under cold running water, shake to dry, and shred finely. Trim and dice the courgettes. Trim the broccoli, removing the thick stalk, and cut into small pieces. Wash and shake dry the greens. Remove any thick stalks and finely shred the green leaves.

2 Pour the stock into a large saucepan. Add the bay leaf and bring to the boil. Add all the vegetables and the peas, bring back to the boil, and cover and simmer for 6 to 7 minutes, until just tender.

3 Remove from the heat and cool for 10 minutes. Discard the bay leaf and transfer to a blender or food processor. Add a few sprigs of basil to the soup, reserving a few leaves for the garnish. Blitz for a few seconds until smooth. Return to the saucepan and season well.

4 When ready to serve, reheat the soup gently until piping hot. Ladle into warm bowls, swirl in some cream, if desired, and top with a dollop of pesto sauce. Serve immediately, sprinkled with a few more basil leaves.

COOK'S NOTE It's easy to make your own pesto: put a peeled clove of garlic in a small blender or food processor and add 15 g (½ oz) fresh basil, 100 g (3½ oz) pine nuts, 50 g (2 oz) freshly grated Parmesan cheese and 4 tablespoons of good-quality extra virgin olive oil. Blend together until smooth and thick. Store in a sealed jar in the refrigerator for up to 10 days. (Serves 4)

FREEZING Make the soup as above, omitting the cream and pesto. Allow to cool, then pack into freezer soup bags or a freezer-proof container. Seal, label and freeze for up to three months. Allow to defrost overnight in the fridge. Reheat gently in a saucepan, stirring, for about 5 minutes until piping hot, and serve as above.

▶ PRODUCE GROWN ON PAGES 24, 34, 36, 48, 54 & 63

Mushroom, garlic and potato soup

SERVES 4–6

1 Tbsp cold-pressed rapeseed oil or other vegetable oil

3 garlic cloves, peeled and chopped

675 g (1½ lb) potatoes, peeled and diced

1 L (1¾ pt) chicken or vegetable stock

Few sprigs of fresh thyme

250 g (9 oz) mushrooms, wiped and chopped

4 Tbsp double cream

Salt and freshly ground black pepper

Pinch of ground nutmeg

An earthy combination of ingredients which blend together perfectly to make a very comforting and tasty light meal. Serve simply with crusty bread and a crisp salad.

1 Heat the oil in a large saucepan until hot and gently cook the garlic for 2 to 3 minutes, until softened but not browned. Add the potato and pour over the stock. Reserving a few sprigs of thyme for the garnish, add a few sprigs to the saucepan, bring to the boil, then cover and simmer gently for 15 minutes.

2 Stir in the mushrooms and continue to cook, covered, for a further 10 minutes, until tender. Remove from the heat and cool for 10 minutes. Discard the thyme sprigs.

3 Transfer to a blender or food processor and blend for a few seconds until smooth. Return to the saucepan, stir in the cream and season to taste with salt, pepper and nutmeg.

4 When ready to serve, reheat until piping hot. Ladle into warm soup bowls and garnish with fresh thyme.

FREEZING Make the soup as above but omit the cream. Allow to cool, then pack into freezer soup bags or a freezer-proof container. Seal, label and freeze for up to three months. Allow to defrost overnight in the fridge. Reheat gently in a saucepan, stirring, for about 5 minutes until piping hot, and continue with the recipe above.

▶ PRODUCE GROWN ON PAGES 22, 30, 56 & 66

Sprouting salad wraps with fresh pea hummus

This is an example of a recipe where the flavour of home-grown produce turns a simple idea into a real feast for the senses. Healthy food has never tasted so good!

1 First make the hummus. Bring a saucepan of lightly salted water to the boil. Add the peas, garlic and ground coriander. Cook for about 5 minutes, until just tender. Drain well, reserving 6 tablespoons of cooking water and cool for 10 minutes.

2 Transfer the cooked peas and garlic to a blender or food processor. Add the reserved cooking water and oil. Blend for a few seconds until smooth. Pile into a heatproof bowl and allow to cool. Season to taste, then cover and chill until required.

3 When ready to serve, wash and shake dry the lettuce leaves. Lay them out flat on the work surface and slice out the central thick core. Spoon a dollop of pea hummus in the centre of each leaf and spread out a little. Top with sprouting seeds, mustard and cress, then some radish and carrot slices. Season to taste.

4 Taking one at a time, fold up the bottom edge of the lettuce to cover half the filling, and then roll carefully from one side to make a tubular wrap. Secure with a cocktail stick. Repeat with all the filled leaves and serve as soon as possible.

COOK'S NOTE 450 g (1 lb) fresh whole peas yield about 225 g (8 oz) shelled. Use this method for making hummus with broad beans as well. If preferred, replace the lettuce leaves with soft flour tortilla wraps or use as a sandwich filling for wholegrain bread. The hummus makes a lovely dip for serving with prepared raw baby vegetables.

FREEZING Not suitable.

SERVES 4

For the pea hummus

Salt

350 g (12 oz) shelled peas

2 garlic cloves, peeled and roughly chopped

2 tsp ground coriander

2 Tbsp cold-pressed rapeseed oil or extra virgin olive oil

For the lettuce wraps

8 large lettuce leaves

Handful of your favourite sprouted seeds, rinsed

Handful of mustard and cress, rinsed

8 radishes, washed, trimmed and thinly sliced

8 baby carrots, scrubbed, trimmed and thinly sliced

Freshly ground black pepper

▶ PRODUCE GROWN ON PAGES 22, 28, 48, 68, 70 & 76

Chilli chorizo and mixed bean salad

SERVES 4

Salt and freshly ground black pepper

200 g (7 oz) shelled broad beans

200 g (7 oz) French beans, topped, tailed and cut into 2.5 cm (1 in) lengths

200 g (7 oz) runner beans, topped, tailed and cut thinly on the diagonal

225 g (8 oz) tomatoes, washed and stalks removed

2 Tbsp white wine vinegar

About 2 tsp caster sugar

350 g (12 oz) chorizo sausage, paper casing removed, and chopped

1 hot red chilli, deseeded and finely chopped

1 orange or red pepper, deseeded and finely chopped

6 spring onions, trimmed and chopped

2 Tbsp freshly chopped parsley

This rich Spanish sausage is a real favourite of mine, and served with freshly cooked beans and a slightly acidic tomato dressing, it makes a truly tasty alternative sausage supper.

1 Bring a saucepan of lightly salted water to the boil and cook the broad beans for 1 minute. Add the French beans and cook for a further minute before adding the runner beans and cooking for 3 to 4 minutes more until just tender. Drain well and rinse in cold running water to cool. Drain again and pat dry with kitchen paper. Set aside.

2 Roughly chop the tomatoes, then blitz in a blender or food processor for a few seconds until smooth. Push through a nylon sieve into a small bowl. Mix in the vinegar, and season with sugar, salt and pepper to taste. Set aside.

3 When ready to serve, put the chorizo in a frying pan and heat gently until the juices run. Raise the heat and stir-fry for 2 to 3 minutes until lightly browned all over. Drain on kitchen paper.

4 Turn the beans into a bowl and mix in the chilli, pepper, spring onions and hot chorizo. Toss in the tomato dressing and serve immediately sprinkled with chopped parsley.

COOK'S NOTE 550 g (1 lb 3½ oz) whole broad beans yield approximately 200 g (7 oz) beans when shelled.

FREEZING Not suitable.

 PRODUCE GROWN ON PAGES 26, 44, 46, 50, 58, 65 & 78

Roast tomato, mascarpone and garlic tart

SERVES 4–6

450 g (1 lb) small tomatoes

375 g pack ready-rolled puff pastry

1 egg, beaten

1 egg yolk

150 g (5½ oz) mascarpone soft cheese

Small bunch of fresh basil

3 garlic cloves, peeled and crushed

Salt and freshly ground black pepper

2 tsp caster sugar

1 Tbsp cold-pressed rapeseed oil or olive oil

25 g (1 oz) pine nuts

25 g (1 oz) piece Parmesan cheese

2 handfuls of your favourite salad leaves, such as rocket or corn salad

A perfect way to enjoy ripe, juicy tomatoes. Adding a little bit of sugar to them before baking helps enhance their natural sweetness even more.

1 Preheat the oven to 200°C (400°F, gas 6). If you are using cherry tomatoes, simply wash and dry them, and remove the stalks. For slightly bigger tomatoes, wash, dry, remove the stalks, and cut in half.

2 Unroll the pastry and place it on a baking tray large enough to hold the pastry (approx 35 x 25 cm / 14 x 10 in), lined with baking parchment. Brush the edges with beaten egg and fold over each side by about 1 cm (½ in). Press to seal and score the edges with a knife. Prick the base all over with a fork, brush lightly with a little beaten egg and bake in the oven for about 10 minutes to 'set' and lightly brown the pastry.

3 Mix the remaining beaten egg with the egg yolk and mascarpone cheese. Finely chop a few sprigs of basil and stir into the cheese mixture along with the garlic and plenty of seasoning.

4 Carefully spoon into the centre of the pastry and spread all over. Arrange the tomatoes on top, cut-side uppermost if halved. Season with black pepper, sprinkle with the sugar and drizzle with rapeseed oil. Sprinkle over the pine nuts and bake for 20 to 25 minutes, or until golden and crisp.

5 Serve warm with shavings of Parmesan cheese and extra basil leaves sprinkled on top of the tart. Accompany with your favourite salad leaves.

FREEZING Omit the Parmesan shavings and basil on top. Allow to cool completely and either leave whole or cut in slices. Open freeze on a tray lined with baking parchment, and then wrap well. Store for up to three months. Reheat on a baking tray from frozen in the oven at 200°C (400°F, gas 6) for 20 to 25 minutes until piping hot, and serve as above.

▶ PRODUCE GROWN ON PAGES 22, 63, 72 & 78

Tempura-style mixed vegetables

This is my version of a Japanese classic. Its simplicity really complements the great tasting freshness and texture of home-grown vegetables.

SERVES 6

2 red or green peppers

150 g (5½ oz) baby corn

1 medium courgette

225 g (8 oz) broccoli

115 g (4 oz) mushrooms, wiped and trimmed

225 g (8 oz) plain flour

2 large egg yolks

½ tsp baking powder

Pinch of salt

2 garlic cloves, peeled and crushed

Vegetable oil for deep-frying

1 First prepare the vegetables. Halve and deseed the peppers, then cut into chunky pieces. Trim the baby corn. Trim the courgette and cut into chunky slices. Remove and discard the thick stalk from the broccoli and cut into thin florets. Cut the mushrooms in half.

2 Bring a large saucepan of water to the boil and blanch the vegetables in a couple of batches for 2 minutes each. Drain and cool under running cold water. Drain well and pat dry with kitchen paper to remove all the water. Transfer to a large bowl and gently toss in 50 g (2 oz) flour.

3 For the batter, in a bowl, mix the egg yolks with 300 ml (½ pt) cold water and sift in the remaining flour and baking powder, beating with a whisk to form a smooth, thick batter. Stir in a pinch of salt and the garlic.

4 When ready to cook, heat the oil for deep-frying to 190°C (375°F). Dip the vegetables in the batter and deep-fry in batches for 4 to 5 minutes until golden. Drain and keep warm whilst cooking the remainder. Best served as quickly as possible after frying, accompanied by soy sauce or other dipping sauce (see Cook's note).

COOK'S NOTE For an authentic dipping sauce, mix together 5 tablespoons of mirin or sweet sherry with the same amount of Japanese soy sauce. Sweeten with 2 teaspoons of clear honey, and serve sprinkled with freshly chopped chives, garlic and chilli if liked.

FREEZING Not suitable.

▶ PRODUCE GROWN ON PAGES 22, 34, 54, 56, 58 & 60

Slow-roast five-spice duck and fresh plum salsa

Fruit and rich meat are an ideal combination, and in this dish you don't even need to cook the fruit first.

1   The day before, wash and pat dry the duck. Put in a shallow dish and rub in the five-spice powder. Place in the fridge, uncovered or loosely covered, for 24 hours before cooking to allow the duck skin to dry out.

2   When ready to cook, preheat the oven to 170°C (325°F, gas 3). Arrange the duck legs on a rack over a roasting tin. Mix the salt and sugar together and sprinkle over the duck skin. Bake in the oven for about 1 hour 40 minutes until the duck is cooked through and skin is richly golden and crisp.

3   Whilst the duck is cooking, mix the plums with the pepper and spring onions. Whisk together the vinegar, honey and sesame oil, and stir into the plum salsa. Cover and chill until required.

4   When ready to serve, drain the duck and shred the meat and skin finely. Mix the coriander, sprouted seeds and Oriental leaves together, and arrange on serving plates. Stir the plum salsa to mix and spoon over the top. Serve the shredded duck on top and accompany with freshly cooked rice or noodles.

COOK'S NOTE Choose the smallest Oriental leaves for this dish to ensure they are tender enough to eat raw.

FREEZING Not suitable.

SERVES 4
4 duck legs
1½ tsp five-spice powder
2 tsp salt
2 tsp caster sugar
300 g (10 oz) ripe plums, halved, stoned and finely chopped
1 small red or yellow pepper, deseeded and finely chopped
4 spring onions, trimmed and finely chopped
2 Tbsp Chinese white rice vinegar
2 tsp clear honey
2 tsp sesame oil
Few sprigs of coriander, roughly chopped
Handful of freshly harvested sprouted seeds, rinsed and roughly chopped
Handful of mizuna or other small Oriental leaf, washed and trimmed

▶ PRODUCE GROWN ON PAGES 26, 40, 58, 63, 76 & 86

Mackerel fish fingers with beetroot and horseradish mash

SERVES 4

350 g (12 oz) small beetroot

675 g (1½ lb) general-purpose potatoes

Salt and freshly ground black pepper

25 g (1 oz) butter

1–2 Tbsp creamed horseradish sauce

4 whole mackerel, cleaned, filleted and skinned

3 Tbsp plain flour

2 medium eggs, beaten

150 g (5½ oz) fresh white breadcrumbs

2 Tbsp each of freshly chopped dill and chives, plus extra to garnish

200 ml (7 fl oz) vegetable oil

Chive flowers and lemon wedges, to garnish

You'll stun everyone when you dish up this vibrant creation, and set taste buds tingling when they take their first mouthful. Try the mash with roast chicken, game or sausages too.

1 Wash the beetroot well, taking care not to cut into the skin or bruise it, and place in a saucepan, unpeeled. Cover with water and bring to the boil. Cook for about 1 hour, until tender. Rinse in cold water until cool enough to handle, then carefully rub off the skin. Mash finely using a fork. Cover and keep warm.

2 About 25 minutes before the beetroot are ready, peel the potatoes and cut them into small chunks. Place in a large saucepan and cover with water. Add a pinch of salt and bring to the boil. Cook for about 10 minutes, until tender. Drain well through a colander or sieve and stand for 10 minutes to dry before returning to the saucepan.

3 Mash the potato with the butter and stir in the beetroot. Add horseradish and seasoning to taste. Cover and keep warm.

4 Slice each mackerel fillet in half lengthways, then in half through the middle, to make short strips of fish. Wash and pat dry. Dust lightly all over with flour. Put the beaten eggs on a plate and season well. On a separate plate, mix together the breadcrumbs and chopped herbs. Coat the fish pieces first in the egg and then the crumbs until well covered.

5 Heat the oil in a medium frying pan and shallow fry the fish in two batches for about 5 minutes, turning occasionally, until lightly golden and crisp. Drain on kitchen paper and keep warm whilst frying the other pieces.

6 To serve, pile the mash on to serving plates and add the fish. Sprinkle with extra chopped herbs to garnish and top with a chive flower. Accompany with wedges of lemon.

FREEZING Not suitable.

▶ PRODUCE GROWN ON PAGES 30, 32, 63, 64 & 102

Brinjal bhaji with minted yoghurt marinated chicken

SERVES 4

500 g (1 lb 2 oz) boneless, skinless chicken, cut into 2.5 cm (1 in) cubes

3 garlic cloves, peeled and crushed

2 tsp mild curry powder

3 Tbsp freshly chopped mint

6 Tbsp whole milk natural yoghurt

Salt and freshly ground black pepper

500 g (1 lb 2 oz) aubergine

3 Tbsp vegetable oil

225 g (8 oz) shallots, peeled and chopped

1 tsp cumin seeds, lightly crushed

1 tsp garam masala

2 sprigs of curry plant

2 bay leaves

300 ml (½ pt) vegetable stock

350 g (12 oz) ripe tomatoes, chopped

2 Tbsp tomato purée

4 Tbsp freshly chopped coriander

I love aubergines, and subsequently this Indian dish is a firm favourite of mine. I always salt aubergines before cooking them so that they become very tender when cooked.

1 Put the chicken in a bowl and mix in 1 garlic clove, the curry powder, chopped mint and yoghurt. Season well. Cover and chill for at least 2 hours. Meanwhile, trim the aubergines and cut into small cubes. Layer in a colander or sieve, sprinkling generously with salt as you go, and set aside for 30 to 40 minutes. Then rinse well and pat dry.

2 Heat the oil in a large saucepan and gently fry the shallots and the remaining garlic with the spices, bay leaves and curry plant for 10 minutes until softened. Add the aubergine and mix well to coat in the fried mixture.

3 Pour over the stock and add the tomatoes, bring to the boil, cover and simmer for about 15 minutes until tender. Stir in the tomato purée and continue to cook, uncovered, for a further 10 minutes until thickened and the liquid is almost absorbed. Discard the bay leaves and curry plant sprigs, and set aside.

4 Preheat the grill to a moderate setting. Thread the chicken pieces on to eight skewers and arrange on a grill rack. Brush with any yoghurt mixture that remains in the bowl.

5 Cook the skewers for about 20 minutes, turning occasionally, until tender and cooked through. Return the aubergine mixture to the heat, adding a little water if it is dry, and reheat, stirring, for 3 to 4 minutes until piping hot. Pile on to warmed serving plates and sprinkle with chopped coriander. Top each portion with two skewers and serve with warm naan bread.

FREEZING Cook and cool the aubergine mixture, then pack into freezer containers. Seal well, label and freeze for up to six months. Defrost overnight in the fridge. Reheat, adding a little water, as above. The chicken skewers are best eaten freshly prepared.

▶ PRODUCE GROWN ON PAGES 22, 26, 52, 63, 64, 65 & 78

Lamb kefta-style with 'creamed' spinach

If the weather's permissible, these Middle Eastern kebabs make a tasty change from the usual barbecue offerings, and the spinach side dish is also very tasty as a cold salad. Chard can be used instead of spinach.

1 Put the lamb in a bowl and add half the garlic, along with the chopped herbs, cumin, 1 teaspoon of salt and some freshly ground black pepper. Mix well with your hands until thoroughly blended.

2 Divide the mixture into 12 portions. Form each into a fat sausage, tapering at the ends. Put on a plate lined with baking parchment, cover and chill for 30 minutes.

3 Meanwhile, melt the butter in a large saucepan and gently fry the shallots and remaining garlic with the spice seeds for 10 minutes until tender and lightly golden. Rinse the spinach and pack into the saucepan whilst still wet. Mix well, cover and allow to cook gently in its own steam for about 5 minutes until well wilted and soft. Drain the spinach, pushing against the side of the colander, then turn on to a board and chop. Return to the saucepan. Cover and set aside.

4 Preheat the grill to a medium/hot setting. Thread three keftas, lengthways, on to four long kebab skewers and arrange on the grill rack. Cook for 6 to 7 minutes on each side until tender, or until cooked to your liking. Keep warm.

5 To finish the spinach, put the saucepan over a low heat and gently reheat, stirring for 2 to 3 minutes. Season well and mix in the yoghurt. Pile on to warm serving plates and top with a lamb skewer. Sprinkle with extra chopped herbs to garnish.

FREEZING The keftas are best frozen raw. Pack between freezer sheets or film in a rigid container. Seal and freeze for up to three months. Defrost in the fridge overnight. Cook as above. The spinach dish is not suitable for freezing.

SERVES 4
675 g (1½ lb) lean minced lamb
4 garlic cloves, peeled and finely chopped
2 Tbsp each freshly chopped coriander and mint, plus extra to garnish
1 tsp ground cumin
Salt and freshly ground black pepper
25 g (1 oz) butter
2 shallots, peeled and finely chopped
2 tsp coriander seeds, crushed
2 tsp cumin seeds, crushed
675 g (1½ lb) spinach, trimmed
2 Tbsp whole milk natural yoghurt

▶ PRODUCE GROWN ON PAGES 22, 26, 42, 63 & 65

Fragrant spiced cauliflower with green rice

SERVES 4

Salt and freshly ground black pepper

250 g (9 oz) basmati rice, rinsed

2 bay leaves

2 sprigs of curry plant

4 Tbsp vegetable oil

3 Tbsp each of freshly chopped dill, parsley and coriander

2 shallots, peeled and finely chopped

2 garlic cloves, peeled and crushed

2.5 cm (1 in) piece root ginger, peeled and finely chopped

1 tsp ground turmeric

6 cardamom pods, lightly crushed

1 tsp garam masala

1 medium cauliflower, trimmed and cut into small florets

1 Tbsp plain flour

300 ml (½ pt) coconut milk

150 ml (¼ pt) vegetable stock

Sprigs of curry plant, to garnish

Naan bread, to serve

This mildly spiced Indian dish makes a delicious main meal on its own, and also a side dish for a main course.

1 Bring a large saucepan of water to the boil. Add 1 teaspoon of salt and the rice. Bring back to the boil, and boil uncovered for 2 minutes, until the rice is only slightly tender and still opaque.

2 Drain and rinse the rice in cold running water. Shake off excess water and put back in the saucepan. Stir in the bay leaves and curry plant sprigs. Flatten the surface and then make indents into the rice with the end of a wooden spoon and drizzle in 2 tablespoon of oil.

3 Cover with a layer of foil and then the saucepan lid. Place over a low heat to cook undisturbed for 30 minutes until tender – the grains on the bottom will begin to crisp. Fork through and discard the bay leaves and curry sprigs. Stir in the chopped fresh herbs and season to taste. Cover and keep warm.

4 Meanwhile, heat the remaining oil in a saucepan and gently fry the shallots, garlic and ginger with the spices, for about 5 minutes, stirring, until softened. Stir in the cauliflower and flour, and cook for 1 minute until evenly coated in the spice mixture.

5 Pour in the coconut milk and stock, bring to the boil, stirring, then cover and simmer gently for 10 to 15 minutes until tender and slightly thickened. Discard the cardamom pods and season well. Spoon the rice on to warm serving plates and ladle over the cauliflower. Garnish with sprigs of curry plant and serve with naan bread.

FREEZING Allow both parts of the recipe to cool, then pack into separate containers. Seal and freeze for up to six months. Defrost in the refrigerator overnight. To reheat the rice, place in a saucepan, add 2 tablespoons of water, cover and put over a low heat, stirring occasionally for about 20 minutes, until piping hot. Reheat the curry in a separate saucepan, stirring for about 5 minutes, until piping hot.

▶ PRODUCE GROWN ON PAGES 22, 26, 38, 63, 64 & 65

Flame-roasted chilli beef burgers and vegetables

Eating out of doors always brings on a hearty appetite, and these meaty burgers and smoky vegetables are the perfect way to satisfy a rumbling tummy.

1 First make the burgers. Put the mince in a bowl and mix in the shallot, parsley, chilli, ketchup and plenty of seasoning. Divide into four equal portions and form each into a chunky burger shape. Put on a plate lined with baking parchment, cover and chill for 30 minutes, or until ready to cook.

2 Meanwhile, put the potatoes in a small saucepan and cover with water. Add a pinch of salt and bring to the boil. Cook for 7 to 8 minutes until just tender. Drain well and set aside to cool.

3 Bring another saucepan of water to the boil, and cook the pepper and baby corn for 3 to 4 minutes until just tender. Drain well and set aside to cool.

4 Thread the prepared vegetables alternately on to four long skewers, except the lettuce. Cover and chill until ready to cook.

5 When you are ready to cook, place the burgers over hot coals and cook for 4 to 5 minutes on each side, or until cooked to your liking. For the vegetables, mix the oil with the smoked paprika, honey and plenty of seasoning, and brush over the vegetables and lettuce. Cook the skewers over hot coals for 4 to 5 minutes, turning and basting frequently, until lightly charred and tender, and the lettuce halves for 1 to 2 minutes on each side. Serve immediately topped with chargrilled sliced red chilli, if liked.

FREEZING The burgers are best frozen raw. Pack between freezer sheets or film in a rigid container. Seal and freeze for up to three months. Defrost in the fridge overnight. Cook as above. The vegetables are not suitable for freezing.

SERVES 4
675 g (1½ lb) lean minced beef
1 shallot, peeled and finely chopped
4 Tbsp freshly chopped parsley
1 red chilli, deseeded and finely chopped
2 Tbsp tomato ketchup
Salt and freshly ground black pepper
12 small same-size potatoes, scrubbed and halved
2 red peppers, deseeded and cut into bite-size pieces
12 baby corn, trimmed
8 spring onions, trimmed to about 5 cm (2 in)
2 small firm lettuce such as Little Gem, trimmed and halved
2 Tbsp cold-pressed rapeseed oil or other vegetable oil
1 tsp smoked paprika
1 Tbsp clear honey
Chargrilled sliced red chilli, to garnish

▶ PRODUCE GROWN ON PAGES 26, 30, 58, 60, 65 & 70

Summer chicken and baby vegetable tray bake

SERVES 4

4 part-boned chicken breasts or chicken quarters

Salt and freshly ground black pepper

4 Tbsp garlic mayonnaise

4 Tbsp fresh white breadcrumbs

2 Tbsp freshly grated Parmesan cheese

3 Tbsp freshly chopped rosemary

225 g (8 oz) baby carrots, trimmed and scrubbed

225 g (8 oz) baby turnips, trimmed and scrubbed

225 g (8 oz) baby leeks, trimmed

500 g (1 lb 2 oz) small new potatoes, scrubbed and sliced

2 Tbsp cold-pressed rapeseed oil or other vegetable oil

Fresh rosemary sprigs, to garnish

A simple meal-in-one that's easy to put together and is packed full of the flavours of the season.

1 Preheat the oven to 200°C (400°F, gas 6). Wash and pat dry the chicken. Season all over. Carefully spread the skin with mayonnaise.

2 Mix the breadcrumbs, cheese and 1 tablespoon of rosemary together and press on top of the mayonnaise to cover completely. Set aside.

3 Meanwhile, halve the carrots and turnips and place in a large bowl. Add the leeks and sliced potatoes, and toss in the oil, the remaining rosemary and plenty of seasoning.

4 Spread out the vegetables evenly on a large baking tray lined with baking parchment. Put the chicken pieces on top and bake in the oven for about 45 minutes, turning the vegetables halfway through, until they are tender and the chicken is cooked through.

5 Drain the chicken and vegetables and serve on warm plates garnished with fresh rosemary.

FREEZING Not suitable.

▶ PRODUCE GROWN ON PAGES 24, 28, 30, 32 & 66

Summer fruit and flower salad

Pick lavender just as the buds have swollen and are about to break into flower for best results. You will only need a few fresh flower buds to give a lovely perfumed flavour to this simple dish.

1 First make the lavender sugar. Wash the fresh lavender and dry well using kitchen paper. Line a board with clear wrap and arrange the lavender on top. Lay a sheet of greaseproof paper on top and gently crush using a rolling pin to extract the oils and the flavour. Carefully pick off the flower buds and mix into the sugar. Set aside.

2 Put the prepared fruit in a serving bowl and sprinkle with the lavender sugar. Cover loosely and stand at room temperature for about 1 hour to allow the flavours to develop.

3 Mix strawberry syrup or cordial into the wine to taste and pour over the fruit salad. Cover and chill for 2 hours. Stand at room temperature for 30 minutes before serving sprinkled with petals and pansies, and accompanied by mascarpone soft cheese or whipped cream.

COOK'S NOTE For a more intense flowery flavour for baking or for longer storage, you need to use dried flower buds. Hang small bundles of freshly picked lavender upside down in a dark, dry place with plenty of air circulation. Put a piece of paper underneath to catch any buds that may fall. The lavender will dry in about 10 days. Rub the flower heads gently with your fingers to remove the dry flower buds. Grind 1 tablespoon of dried buds in a spice grinder along with 1 tablespoon of granulated sugar until finely ground. Stir in a further 175 g (6 oz) sugar, place in a clean jar, seal and store for at least three days before using. Keeps for up to six months.

FREEZING Not suitable.

SERVES 4

For the lavender sugar

2 sprigs freshly picked lavender, green foliage removed

2 Tbsp caster sugar

For the fruit

450 g (1 lb) assorted berries and currants, such as blackberries, blackcurrants, white currants, cherries, blueberries, gooseberries, raspberries, small strawberries and redcurrants, prepared and washed

2–4 Tbsp strawberry syrup (see page 140) or readymade berry cordial

150 ml (¼ pt) dry rosé wine

Few calendula petals and small pansies, to decorate

▶ PRODUCE GROWN ON PAGES 63–5, 82, 88 & 92–8

Gooseberry and pudding wine jellies

A light, softly set dessert that makes a fruity finale to any meal. Delicious topped with a good dollop of clotted cream.

SERVES 4

500 g (1 lb 2 oz) green gooseberries, topped and tailed

75–115 g (3–4 oz) caster sugar

Juice of ½ lemon

5 sheets of leaf gelatine

150 ml (¼ pt) white dessert wine

4 Tbsp clotted cream

Few edible flower petals, pansies and mint leaves, to decorate

1 Put the gooseberries in a saucepan with 75 g (2½ oz) sugar. Add 4 tablespoons of water, heat gently, stirring until the sugar dissolves. Raise the heat, bring to the boil, cover and simmer gently for about 5 minutes until very soft.

2 Transfer to a blender or food processor and blitz until smooth. Push through a nylon sieve to make a smooth purée (you need approximately 600 ml / 1 pt). Mix in the lemon juice, taste and add more sugar if required. Set aside to cool.

3 Cut each leaf of gelatine into small pieces and place in a heatproof bowl. Spoon over 4 tablespoons of cold water and leave aside to soak for 10 minutes. Melt the gelatine in the bowl over a pan of simmering water and set aside to cool.

4 Stir the wine and gelatine into the gooseberry purée and pour into small tumblers or wine glasses. Chill for at least 4 hours until set. Serve topped with a dollop of clotted cream and decorated with flower petals, pansies and mint.

COOK'S NOTE You can follow this method to make jellies using other berry fruits and currants; just adjust the amount of sugar to taste.

FREEZING Not suitable.

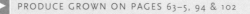

▶ PRODUCE GROWN ON PAGES 63–5, 94 & 102

Chilled rhubarb with warm zabaglione foam

SERVES 4

For the rhubarb

350 g (12 oz) rhubarb stalks, leaves removed

115 g (4 oz) caster sugar

For the foam

4 medium free-range or organic egg yolks

4 Tbsp caster sugar

4 Tbsp Marsala wine

This recipe sounds complicated but it's actually very straightforward. You do need to make the foam at the last minute if you want to serve it warm, otherwise prepare in advance and serve cold. It's great with just about any fruit.

1 Trim and cut the rhubarb into 10 cm (4 in) lengths. Place the sugar in a medium frying pan with a lid and pour over 120 ml (4 fl oz) water. Heat gently, stirring until dissolved, then bring to the boil and simmer for 3 minutes.

2 Add the rhubarb to the pan, laying the pieces side by side. Bring back to the boil, cover and simmer for 3 minutes. Carefully turn the rhubarb over, re-cover and cook for a further 3 to 4 minutes until just cooked. Remove from the heat and allow to cool completely. Transfer to a serving dish, cover and chill for at least 2 hours before serving.

3 For the foam, put the egg yolks in a heatproof bowl with the sugar and whisk until very thick, pale and creamy. Whisk in the Marsala.

4 Place the bowl over a saucepan of gently simmering (not boiling) water and whisk continuously, scraping round the bowl from time to time as the mixture begins to thicken. Keep whisking until the mixture thickens into soft peaks – but be careful because overcooking will result in scrambled egg!

5 Either serve warm, spooned over the chilled rhubarb, or remove from the water and allow to cool, then cover and chill until required.

FREEZING Not suitable.

 PRODUCE GROWN ON PAGE 100

Chunky apple and pear fritters

When you put a fork through the light batter casing, the fresh fruit filling will ooze with juice and natural flavour. Serve simply sprinkled with cinnamon-flavoured caster sugar and a dollop of whipped cream or ice cream. Alternatively, try my cranberry sauce with the fritters (see Cook's note).

SERVES 4
2 eating apples
2 ripe pears
100 g (3½ oz) plain flour
Pinch of salt
1 medium egg, beaten
150 ml (¼ pt) whole milk
Vegetable oil for deep frying
4 Tbsp caster sugar
½ tsp ground cinnamon

1 Peel and core the apples and pears, and cut into large slices about 1 cm (½ in) thick. Sift half the flour over a large plate and gently toss the fruit into it to cover lightly all over. Set aside.

2 Sieve the remaining flour and salt in a small bowl and gradually mix in the egg and milk to form a smooth batter.

3 Heat the oil for deep frying to 190°C (375°F). Dip the slices of fruit in the batter and fry five or six slices at a time for 3 to 4 minutes until crisp and golden. Drain on kitchen paper.

4 To serve, mix the sugar and cinnamon together and sprinkle over the fruit fritters. Serve immediately with cream or ice cream.

COOK'S NOTE Put 175 g (6 oz) prepared and washed cranberries in a saucepan and pour over 150 ml (¼ pt) freshly squeezed orange juice or cold water. Bring to the boil and simmer gently for 5 minutes until the berries start to pop open and soften. Remove from the heat and stir in approximately 75 g (2½ oz) caster sugar to taste. Serve hot or cold with the fritters. The sauce is also good served cold with roast meats and game.

FREEZING Not suitable.

▶ PRODUCE GROWN ON PAGES 80, 84 & 90

Festive kumquat and ginger trifle

SERVES 6

300 g (10 oz) kumquats, washed and stalks removed

5 Tbsp caster sugar

4 Tbsp ginger wine

1 tsp finely grated orange rind

175 g (6 oz) piece Jamaican ginger cake or similar

425 g can custard

300 ml (½ pt) double cream

Edible silver and gold balls, to decorate

Not usually one of my favourite puddings, but this version would make it on my alternative Christmas dessert Top Ten. It also works well at other times of the year with poached pears, fresh raspberries or stewed rhubarb.

1 Slice the kumquats thinly and remove as many seeds as possible. Put the sliced fruit in a saucepan with 6 tablespoons of water and 3 tablespoons of sugar. Heat gently, stirring, until the sugar dissolves, then bring to the boil, cover and simmer gently for 8 to 10 minutes until very tender.

2 Add the ginger wine and orange rind. Mix well and then pour off 75 ml (2½ fl oz) juices into a heatproof jug, and add the remaining sugar to it, stirring until dissolved. Allow the fruit and the juice to cool.

3 Cut the ginger cake into bite-size pieces and put in the bottom of six tumblers or individual bowls. Spoon over the cooled fruit, then pour over the custard. Cover and chill until ready to serve.

4 Just before serving, whip the cream until just beginning to thicken. Still whisking, pour in the reserved cooled juice, and continue whisking until softly peaking. Pile on top of the custard and sprinkle with edible silver and gold balls to serve.

FREEZING Not suitable.

▶ PRODUCE GROWN ON PAGE 102

Sugar-crusted courgette, lemon and lime loaf cake

SERVES 10

3 medium eggs, beaten

225 ml (8 fl oz) sunflower oil

250 g (9 oz) caster sugar

200 g (7 oz) self-raising flour

¾ tsp baking powder

75 g (2½ oz) ground almonds

Finely grated rind of 1 lemon

Finely grated rind of 1 lime

175 g (6 oz) yellow or green courgettes, trimmed and grated

3 Tbsp Demerara sugar

A great cake with a hidden ingredient that helps keep it moist. Leave it to stand for 24 hours and the cake will have more flavour. Use grated carrot instead of the courgette if preferred.

1 Preheat the oven to 180°C (350°F, gas 4). Grease and line a 900 g (2 lb) loaf tin. In a mixing bowl, whisk together the eggs, oil and caster sugar until smooth and well blended.

2 Sieve over the flour and baking powder, and add the ground almonds, and lemon and lime rind. Carefully mix the ingredients together until well combined. Fold in the courgette.

3 Pile the mixture into the prepared tin and smooth the top. Sprinkle thickly with Demerara sugar. Bake in the oven for about 1 hour, until golden and firm in the centre (test with a skewer inserted into the centre; it should come out clean if the cake is cooked properly). Leave to cool in the tin for 30 minutes, then transfer to a wire rack to cool completely. Wrap and store for a day before serving.

4 Slice thickly and serve with a cup of tea, or serve as a pudding with pouring cream and berry fruits.

FREEZING Cool thoroughly, then wrap well and freeze for up to six months. Allow to defrost at room temperature in the freezer wrappings.

▶ PRODUCE GROWN ON PAGES 54 & 102

Raspberry and white chocolate pancakes

SERVES 4

125 g (4½ oz) self-raising flour

1 Tbsp caster sugar

2 medium eggs, separated

250 ml (9 fl oz) whole milk

115 g (4 oz) fresh raspberries, washed and lightly mashed

50 g (2 oz) white chocolate chips

1 tsp good quality vanilla extract

25 g (1 oz) unsalted butter

Extra fresh raspberries and vanilla sugar, to serve

Feathery-light in texture with the tanginess of fresh fruit and decadence of molten chocolate. Serve straight out of the pan to enjoy them at their best.

1 Sift the flour and sugar into a bowl and make a well in the centre. Add the egg yolks, pour in the milk, and gradually work into the flour using a whisk. Beat until thick and smooth but taking care not to over-mix.

2 In a clean, grease-free bowl, whisk the egg whites until stiff and carefully fold into the batter using a large metal spoon, along with the raspberries, chocolate chips and vanilla.

3 Heat a quarter of the butter in a small 18 cm (7 in) diameter frying pan until melted and bubbling. Ladle in a quarter of the batter and cook over a low to moderate heat for 4 to 5 minutes, until bubbles appear on the surface. Turn over and cook for a further 2 to 3 minutes, until golden and puffed up.

4 Turn the pancake out on to a wire rack lined with a clean tea towel and baking parchment. Cover to keep warm. Repeat this to use up all the batter, re-buttering the pan and stirring the batter each time. Delicious served with extra fresh raspberries and vanilla sugar to sprinkle over.

FREEZING Allow to cool and stack between layers of baking parchment. Place in a freezer bag and seal well, or wrap well in foil, or place in a sealed freezer-proof container. Freeze for up to six months. Allow to defrost at room temperature in the freezer wrappings. To reheat, arrange on a baking sheet lined with baking parchment. Cover with foil and place in a preheated oven at 190°C (375°F, gas 5) for 5 to 6 minutes until piping hot.

▶ PRODUCE GROWN ON PAGE 96

Beetroot and apple chutney

A simple preserve which cuts down on the more lengthy processes involved with traditional chutney making. Keep unopened for 48 hours to allow the flavours to develop.

1 Put the bay leaf, chilli and spices in a small piece of muslin and tie together with clean string. Place in a saucepan. Pour over the vinegar and add the garlic, shallots, apple and sugar.

2 Bring to the boil, stirring occasionally, and simmer gently for 10 minutes, until softened. Allow to cool, then discard the spice bag.

3 Put the beetroot in a bowl and stir in the cold vinegar mixture. Season with salt and spoon into cold, sterilized jars and seal well (see Preservation tips on page 138). Store in the fridge for a couple of days before opening and use within two weeks.

COOK'S NOTE To cook fresh beetroot, wash the roots well, taking care not to cut into the skin or bruise it, and place in a saucepan, unpeeled. Cover with water and bring to the boil. Cook for 1 to 2 hours, depending on size. Drain and cool in cold water until you are able to handle them, then carefully rub off the skin.

FREEZING Not suitable.

MAKES ABOUT 750 g (1 lb 10 oz)
1 bay leaf
1 small dried chilli
Small piece of cinnamon stick
½ tsp black peppercorns, crushed
1 tsp coriander seeds, crushed
225 ml (8 fl oz) white wine vinegar
2 garlic cloves, peeled and crushed
2 shallots, peeled and finely chopped
1 eating apple, peeled, cored and finely chopped
3 Tbsp granulated sugar
500 g (1 lb 2 oz) peeled, cooked beetroot, grated (see Cook's note)
1 tsp salt

▶ PRODUCE GROWN ON PAGES 22, 26, 32, 63 & 80

No-fuss berry jam

MAKES ABOUT 500g (1 lb 2 oz)

250 g (9 oz) caster sugar

250 g (9 oz) fresh, ripe, unblemished berries, washed and patted dry

50 ml (2 fl oz) liquid pectin

An uncooked, soft-textured fresh fruit spread that works with blueberries, blackberries, strawberries and raspberries.

1 Put the sugar in a saucepan and place over a low heat. Heat gently for about 10 minutes, stirring occasionally, until hot. Take care not to melt or burn the sugar as it heats. Meanwhile, put the berries in a bowl and crush with a fork or potato masher. Stir in the pectin.

2 Mix the hot sugar into the crushed berries for a couple of minutes until the sugar has melted. Spoon into sterilized jars (see below) to within 5 mm ($\frac{1}{4}$ in) of the top and seal well. Cool then keep in the fridge for 48 hours before using (up to one month unopened). Once opened, eat within two weeks. For freezing, follow the instructions above but pour into clean freezer containers, leaving a 1 cm ($\frac{1}{2}$ in) space at the top for expansion during freezing. Cover and chill for 48 hours, then freeze for up to six months. Defrost overnight in the fridge and store as above.

PRESERVING TIPS

- For successful preserving you need to make sure everything is thoroughly clean and well sealed to prevent spoilage.
- **Sterilizing jars and bottles:** use sound glass containers and bottles with no chips or cracks. Wash thoroughly with mild detergent and rinse well. Put them open-side up in a deep saucepan, cover with boiling water, bring to the boil and boil for 10 minutes. Lift out with tongs and leave to drain upside down on a thick clean towel. Place on a baking tray lined with a few sheets of kitchen paper and keep warm in the oven set on its lowest setting until ready to fill.
- **Sealing:** as soon as the preserve is in the jar, place a waxed paper circle directly on the top of the jam. Either top with a screw-on lid or seal tightly with a transparent jam pot cover and an elastic band. If you have lots of jars to fill, it is better to allow the preserve to cool completely in the jars before sealing with waxed paper circles and lids. Avoid covering semi-warm preserves as too much condensation will form and this could encourage mould to grow during storage. For chutneys, pickles and other preserves with vinegar, make sure the seals used are non-corrosive. Half-filled jars should be cooled, sealed and kept in the fridge, and eaten as soon as possible.

▶ PRODUCE GROWN ON PAGES 88, 96 & 98

Fresh strawberry syrup

ABOUT 400 ml (13½ fl oz)

900 g (2 lb) ripe fresh strawberries, washed and hulled

115 g (4 oz) caster sugar

2 Tbsp freshly squeezed lemon juice

A refreshing way to enjoy the fragrant flavour of one of our favourite berries. Pour over ice cream or dilute with chilled spring water – great added to fruit salads, cocktails and punches!

1 Place the strawberries in a blender or food processor and blitz for a few seconds until smooth.

2 Pour through a jelly bag or a large nylon sieve lined with a sheet of clean muslin, suspended over a clean bowl and leave in a cool place (or fridge) for up to 24 hours to allow the fruit to strain thoroughly. Don't push or squeeze the fruit as this will make a cloudy juice.

3 Pour the juice into a non-reactive saucepan and add the sugar. (Note: this quantity of fruit yields about 300 ml / ½ pt juice. For larger quantities, measure the juice and add 225 g (8 oz) sugar per 600 ml / 1 pt juice.)

4 Heat gently, stirring over a low heat just until the sugar dissolves – do not boil. Remove from the heat and stir in the lemon juice. Stand for 5 minutes before pouring through a funnel into hot sterilized bottles to within 2 cm (¾ in) of the top (see Preservation tips on page 138) and seal tightly with a non-corrosive lid. Store in the fridge for up to two weeks.

5 To preserve the syrup for long-term storage, loosen the seal slightly. Stand in a deep, narrow saucepan on a trivet and wedge with cloths to prevent the bottles touching each other and the sides of the pan – I find an asparagus steamer good for this purpose. Fill the saucepan with warm water to just cover the bottles and cover with a lid. Heat to simmering point – 88°C (190°F) – and maintain a steady simmer for 20 minutes.

6 Carefully lift the bottles on to a board, seal tightly and cool. Store in a cool, dark, dry place for up to six months. Once opened, store in the fridge and use within two weeks.

FREEZING Not suitable.

▶   PRODUCE GROWN ON PAGES 98 & 102

Useful addresses

SEED MERCHANTS/PLANT SUPPLIERS/GARDEN CENTRES

Chiltern Seeds
www.chilternseeds.co.uk

Dobbies Garden Centres plc
www.dobbies.com

E W King & Co Ltd
www.kingsseeds.co.uk

Edwin Tucker & Sons Ltd
www.edwintucker.co.uk

Hillier Garden Centres/Nurseries Ltd
www.hillier.co.uk

Mr Fothergill's Seeds Ltd
www.fothergills.co.uk

Notcutts Garden Centres
www.notcutts.co.uk

O A Taylor & Sons Bulbs Ltd
www.taylors-bulbs.com

Samuel Dobie & Son
www.dobies.co.uk

Sutton Seeds
www.sutton-seeds.co.uk

Westland Horticulture Ltd
www.gardenhealth.com

Wyevale Garden Centres
www.wyevale.co.uk

ASSOCIATIONS, ORGANIZATIONS AND WEBSITES

Garden organic/Henry Doubleday Research Association
www.gardenorganic.co.uk

GrowVeg
www.growveg.com

The Royal Horticultural Society
www.rhs.org.uk

The Soil Association
www.soilassociation.org

Bibliography

Berry, Susan *Kitchen Harvest* (Frances Lincoln, 2002)

Food from your Garden (Reader's Digest, 1977)

Hawkins, Kathryn *Fruit and Vegetable Grower's Cookbook* (New Holland, 2009)

Hawkins, Kathryn *The Allotment Cookbook* (New Holland, 2007)

Hessayon, Dr D G *The Vegetable & Herb Expert* (Expert Books, 2000)

Purnell, Bob *Crops in Pots* (Hamlyn, 2007)

Raven, Sarah *The Great Vegetable Plot* (BBC Books, 2005)

Royal Horticultural Society *Encyclopedia of Gardening* (Dorling Kindersley, reprint, 1994)

Acknowledgements

From the early spring of 2009 until early winter of the same year, I spent many a long hour raising and looking after the plants for this book. I'd like to apologize to my family and friends for neglecting them in favour of my fruit and veg during this time, and at least now the book's in print they will be able to see what I was up to! I would like to thank photographer Stuart MacGregor for his dedication throughout the project and for his fine attention to detail which has given this book such superior images. My thanks also to Ian Garlick for the lovely food photography.